# CONTENTS

C000246296

*This book covers a lot more than just carp rigs*

Hello and welcome to the second book in which the Fox Carp Team show you some of their latest rigs and associated ideas which have helped them put more carp on the bank. My name is Ken Townley and over the course of the following chapters I will guide you through some of the most advanced tactics in modern carp fishing.

This book covers a lot more than just carp rigs. It is more of an in depth guide to carp fishing, not just rigs. We will look at more advanced rigs designed to give you the edge and we will also look at an aspect of your tackle that many anglers take too much for granted, namely, the area extending behind the lead to the bank.

In addition, the book will cover bite detection showing you how to fine tune your gear and gain the maximum sensitivity. Other chapters will cover proven carp rigs such as the new wave of stiff rigs, hinged rigs, helicopter rigs, lead core rigs and pop-up rigs. We'll also examine the pros and cons of using backleads.

It is important for the modern carp angler to think not just about the final section of his gear – the End Zone as we call it – but also at what is going on above the lead. Choice of main line is something that often causes confusion so we will take an in-depth look at modern braids, not forgetting monofilament and the new fluorocarbon main lines.

PVA in all its forms plays a very important part in today's carp fishing so we will be covering in detail the use of PVA funnels, bags, tape and string and will even cover streamlining your PVA end gear for maximum range. To be honest, the use of PVA could fill a book in its own right and unfortunately we are rather restricted on space. However, we will be able to put across some general pointers and ideas to give the reader a good start which will hopefully point you in the right direction.

Spodding is equally important in our sport so the book will detail the type of spods that are available and which perform best for a particular application. Obviously some spods are better suited to laying down a big bed of bait, while others are designed for smaller carpets, possibly at greater ranges. Spod rods too will come under the spotlight.

In Chapter 8 Fox consultant, Ian 'Chilly' Chillcott gives us his thoughts on bait. Using the best tackle and latest rigs certainly doesn't do your chances of catching any harm, but if the fish aren't interested in eating the bait you put in front of them it doesn't matter how good your gear is, you still won't catch!

In the first book in this series, published in November 2004, we outlined the Fox philosophy on rigs, looking at half a dozen set-ups guaranteed to get your buzzers screaming and your pulses racing. However, as in any walk of life, carp fishing moves on so in this book we will be looking at some of the developments to hit the scene in the past twelve months.

Throughout the book we will be using the new range of accessories from the Fox stable. All the items from the smallest rig ring to the strongest leadcore have been designed to give the angler an advantage when constructing modern rigs. Many of the changes may seem very slight: a Teflon non-reflective finish on a rig ring may seem fastidious to many, but, the smallest things can make the biggest difference, and nowhere is this more

*"the smallest things can make the biggest difference, and nowhere is this more true than carp fishing"*

true than with carp fishing. We have got some great ideas lined up for you in these pages and we feel sure each and every one of you will gain a valuable insight into how the Fox Carp Team approaches its fishing.

When the guys at Fox first decided to write this series of books we all sat down and put our heads together. At first sight the project seemed fairly straight forward but then we thought about it a bit more and realised that it was a much more demanding task than we had first imagined. Rigs have acquired an almost mystical status these days; it's almost as if modern carp anglers think that they are the only thing that matters. So before we get down to the nuts and bolts of carp rigs and carp fishing in general it is probably a good idea to get a general overview of the subject.

Rigs are evolving all the time yet it would be wrong to write off any rig simply because it seems old fashioned. Don't make the mistake of becoming a dedicated follower of fashion without knowing the reasons why! Sure, some of the rigs in this book will take your fishing to another level, but don't loose sight of the fact that probably more fish are caught on Jim Gibbinson's Line Aligner Rig than just about any other, and that simple knotless knot presentations account for thousands of carp every year. By all means keep your finger on the pulse but don't go chopping and changing rigs simply for the sake of it. If it's not broke, don't fix it!

One more point before we start. Though the last book was called the Fox Guide to Carp Rigs, as this second book came together we realised that the information and diversity of material meant it was going to cover a great deal more information than just rigs. That is why this year we have changed the name of the book. We could easily have called it The Fox Guide to Carp Rigs – 2, but that would not convey what this book is all about. Instead we have called it the Fox Guide to Modern Carp Fishing. We hope you like it!

**STEVE SPURGEON**
'This guide has been designed to give you, the reader the best technical information possible. All aspects of modern carp fishing have been covered including spodding, PVA bag fishing, bite detection, knot tying and rigs. There is no doubting that this book will help you to catch more carp!'

**TOM MAKER**
'The Fox Guide to Modern Carp Fishing is packed to the brim with excellent diagrams, pictures and technical sequences that will only help to make you a better carp angler. Whether you are newcomer to carp fishing or have been in the game for a while you cannot fail but learn some new and exciting tactics here.'

**IAN CHILLCOTT**
'This highly educational book will prove invaluable to anglers looking to improve on carp tactics and skills or learn new strings to their bow. A huge range of subject material is meticulously covered in great detail, while also being easy to digest and understand.'

Rigs...what a subject! It means different things to different people and were you to put ten carp anglers in a room and ask them to talk about rigs it's doubtful if any two of them could agree. Sure, rigs are a vital part of the carp fishing jigsaw, but there is so much more to successful fishing than rigs alone. So before we go any further it is important to put the whole subject of carp rigs into some kind of perspective.

Many young carp anglers or those who are newcomers to carp fishing seem to think that the rig is the be-all and end-all of carp fishing. Well that simply isn't so. Always keep in the back of your mind that even the best rig in the world, coupled with the finest bait known to Man will not catch a carp if it is cast into No Carp Bay! On the other hand, a pile of junk for a rig and a load of old rubbish for a bait at least stands a chance if it is cast into Carp City.

No matter how crafty your rig may be, or how attractive your bait, you also need to be able to find the fish in order to reap the rewards that the rig and bait have given you. Keep your eye on the ball rigwise, by all means, but don't let rigs rule your head. They are just a part of the overall plan to put a carp on the bank; they are not the sole consideration.

For instance, most of the top anglers, especially those in the Fox Carp Team, accept that there is a strong relationship between bait and rig, regarding one as inseparable from the other. However, many less experienced anglers seem to think that the rig is king and the bait is way down the pecking order, a thinking we consider to be greatly flawed.

It is no coincidence that the Fox Carp Team members all use what they consider to be the best carp baits going as they know that the rig is only as good as the bait that is on it. The harder a carp feeds in your swim, the easier it is to catch as it will be full of confidence, with its guard down. When it is feeding like this it will be much more likely to make a mistake on the hookbait. Remember, a confident carp is a catchable carp and one that is turned on by the bait will make more mistakes than one that is indifferent towards it.

Now that there are so many great baits out there on the market, from Mainline and Nutrabaits to name just two, we are all able to give the carp a bait that they will eat with confidence and this makes catching them just that little bit easier. You have got to make them have it, and you can't do that with a rubbish bait. Once you have the bait sorted the rig then comes to the fore and in this book we will give you enough ideas about rigs to satisfy even the biggest rig addict.

For the most part the guys at Fox tend to keep things simple as far as rigs are concerned, turning to the more complex rigs only when they are absolutely necessary. For the most part the carp that inhabit our lakes and rivers can be fooled with comparatively basic rigs and while it is true that the more pressured waters may demand something a bit more advanced, before turning to such a set-up it is as well to judge the overall angling situation and pick your rig accordingly. If for instance you arrive at a deserted, overgrown lake with no signs of previous angling activity, the chances are that a basic rig will suffice. However, if you arrive to be confronted by a bivvy city, it's fair to assume that you are going to need something a bit trickier! However, it is pointless to go chopping and changing rigs left, right and centre simply for the sake of it.

An angler who uses tried and tested set-ups is likely to be much more successful in the long run than one who is always looking for the 'ultimate' rig, continuously switching from one rig to another without giving any of them a chance to show their mettle. For instance, as a starting point the successful angler will probably use one rig for pop-ups, another for critically balanced bottom baits, and a third for standard bottom baits. He may use a more advanced rig from time to time, but only when he thinks it is justified.

## "most top carp anglers... are more likely to move than change their rig"

In fact, most of the top carp anglers have so much faith in their presentation that they are more likely to move if they are blanking rather than change their rigs. Why, you ask? Well nine times out of ten if they are not getting takes it is more to do with poor location than poor rig. If you have faith in your rig but are not catching it could mean that you are fishing the proverbial No Carp Bay and a move is much more likely to produce than a change of rig. However, anglers make the mistake of blaming their rig above all else, refusing to acknowledge a weakness in other areas of their fishing.

If you are lucky enough to be able to watch carp in their natural environment you will know that you can learn a great deal about everyday carp fishing by simply looking in on the fish and watching how they react to rigs and baits. There's no more pleasing sight in carping that to watch fish eating your bait with gusto. It takes away all the guesswork and allows your confidence to bloom. Seeing how carp approach a carpet of bait can open doors that would otherwise remain closed to you and it is a real eye opener to see fish feeding and reacting to baiting situations. You can then assess your rig and maybe fine-tune it to cope with the way the carp are feeding.

It is often stated that hard pressured carp are rig-shy but it this really the case? Yes, a carp may be able to identify the hookbait from the way it behaves but this doesn't mean it doesn't pick it up. From my own observations I have watched carp pick up a hookbait a dozen or more times without showing any sign of suspicion. This tells me that the carp isn't shy of the rig or hooklink or the lead weight but that the rig itself is not performing. A more effective rig would have put that fish on the bank.

If you can find a quiet out-of-the-way spot on a lake where it is possible to look in on the carp to see how they feed and how they react to bait and rigs you will learn a great deal more than by trial and error. I am very fortunate in that there are many gin-clear lakes near my home that contain good carp and I have been able to watch them feeding and assess their reactions to both bait and rigs. Believe me, sometimes it is a miracle we catch at all! But I must make the point here that they are not always, as we so often assume, rejecting the hookbait because they are suspicious of it. Were that the case they'd clear off out of the swim at a vast rate of knots. However, for the most part they calmly spit out the bait and continue to feed as if nothing had happened. They will even pick it up again, and again. Eventually they realise there is something about it they don't like and will stop picking it up but they don't necessarily spook from the area. And even if they do flee you'd be surprised how often they return to the swim to resume feeding. Even the so-called 'super rigs' are not 100% successful in the natural environment that a carp calls home. Too often anglers accept what they think might be happening as fact, without confirming what is actually happening.

---

M y colleagues in the Fox Carp Team, especially those that fish on the continent, seem to pick relatively simple rigs. Guys like Andre Akkermans, Mark Noorman, and Jocelyn Dupre, Roberto Ripamonti and Sandro di Ceasare choose tough, meaty end gear in which they have total confidence. They don't have rig boards or wallets containing hundreds of different permutations. In fact if you compared their tackle boxes or looked at their rig wallets you would probably find the same basic rigs in each one!

To a certain extent the same is true of the UK members of the Team. Ask Steve Spurgeon or Ian Chillcott, Chris Rose or Tom Maker, Andy Little or myself our thoughts on rigs and I doubt if we'd be far apart. Simplicity coupled with efficiency is the name of the game and though each one of us will have a favourite rig, I doubt if there will be much disagreement among us as to which are the best. Generally speaking our rigs are uncluttered, not too complicated and most importantly of all: proven fish catchers that have worked well for us well in the past. However, we will not hesitate to use something a bit more complex or different if we feel it is justified, practical and likely to be better than anything tried so far.

You too should be prepared to ring the changes if you think a rig is not working, but please don't do so simply for the sake of it. Keep things in perspective and don't make the mistake of blaming the rig above all else when your lack of success may be due to something else that you might have overlooked or miscalculated. If you are in the right spot, using a first class bait that the carp really want to eat the rig doesn't always need to be over complicated.

The point is that once the particular Pandora's box that held the basic hair rig was opened everything that followed was just a variation on a theme. You can be as complicated or as simple in your choice of rig as you like but at the end of the day it's just a hookbait on a hair that is attached in some way to the hook.

## "Rigs are perhaps the most contentious issue in modern carp fishing"

Rigs are perhaps the most contentious issue in modern carp fishing and we all should take account of different anglers' preferences. Some of us just like to get a fish on the bank. If it's a lump, all well and good, but if it's a more modest fish, well that's good too! Not all of us are big fish or bust anglers. However, it must be accepted that there are plenty of record chasers out there and they may have completely different ideas about rigs, ideas that may actually be big-carp specific. This can cloud the rigs issue if an inexperienced angler tries to take account of what appears to be conflicting advice coming from several totally different viewpoints.

No rig is going to perform identically on every single carp water. There are too many imponderables to consider for that to be the case. Water depth and clarity, silt and mud, weed growth, the presence of gravel; all these need to be taken into consideration on an individual basis. I doubt if anyone can give a definitive answer to the question of which rig is best for all lakes regardless of type. It's a matter of horses for courses.

Nowadays all kinds of weird and wonderful permutations of the original hair rig have been invented. In fact, there are so many rigs about it is small wonder the newcomer to the sport becomes totally confused by it all. When the fishing is slow it is all too common to see an inexperienced or uncertain angler try rig after rig in a vain attempt to get a take. As one rig comes off and another goes on and the runs still fail to materialise his frustration grows, yet in all probability his lack of success has nothing to do with his rig. Nevertheless, the frantic search for the 'ultimate rig' continues. So what can you do to eliminate indecision and doubt? Well the old adage advises us to Keep It Simple, and this is as good a place to start as any. Yes, you may have read all the rig books and seen all the slide shows and workshops and you've probably bought all that modern carp fishing technology can offer, however, it is far better to start off by keeping things as simple as you can, only going on to more advanced rig concepts if the simple things let you down. After all, if you start at the top of the rig tree there's only one way you can go after that...Down!

Many anglers make the mistake of thinking in terms of their rig as meaning the hook/hair set up in isolation.

While it was true that in the early days of the hair rig the hair itself was the determining factor, these days you need to pay more attention to detail. Carp are now coming under increasing pressure as more and more anglers turn to the sport, and with technical information becoming ever more widely available that pressure is growing daily. Because of this the thinking angler will not just be considering his hook and hair arrangement, but will pay strict attention to the whole terminal set up including the hooklink, swivel, lead and the way it is attached, and the tackle behind the lead.

In the following chapters we are going to look in detail at some of the problems we may encounter in our everyday fishing and examine ways to counter them, looking at several rigs in detail, including how to tie them, and explaining how and more importantly why they work.

# *CHAPTER 1*

## *Proven Carp Rigs*

*"Pop-ups were devised way back in the 1980's"*

No doubt you all know what we mean by a pop-up hookbait but for those who are not sure it is any hookbait that has built-in buoyancy that requires a certain amount of counter-weight to pin it down on the lakebed.

Pop-ups were 'invented', for want of a better word, way back in the early 1980s. At the time, the guys who were on pressured lakes such as Savay knew that their quarry was growing increasingly wary of standard presentations involving bottom baits and many felt that the carp had even become adept at identifying the hookbait. One of the first moves towards the use of buoyant baits came about with the invention of the D-Rig. Savay syndicate member Roger Smith devised the D-Rig which represented a radical departure from the standard hair. Roger's idea was to mount the bait on a sliding ring that was free to run along a section of nylon that was attached to the hook in a D formation. The idea was that when a

carp picked up the bait and tried to eject it, the bait would fly out but the hook would stay behind. After a bit of trial and error Roger hit upon the idea of using the rig with a buoyant hookbait and this created a really deadly set up.

Roger's D-Rig was a real step forward and it really brought pop-ups into the spotlight. However, it has to be said that at the time the concept of a popped-up hookbait came about simply as an alternative presentation and was not devised for any practical reason such as the presence of weed or silt.

Since its innovation the D rig has seen many variations on Roger's original theme and all manner of pop-up rigs now rely on a D system of some kind. Over the years many pop-up presentations have been proposed and some take the concept on a few steps. It is probably fair to say at least 50% of all pop-up rigs rely on some form of D-style presentation.

Over the past decade pop-ups have become so popular that you could be forgiven for thinking that they were the only presentation worth mentioning! You may also get the impression that all the top anglers who write for the magazines are on pop-ups. Well, that isn't the case. As in all aspects of carp fishing, the choice of rig needs to be carefully assessed on a lake to lake basis and it may well be that on some lakes pop-ups are less effective than on others.

All the Fox Carp Team use pop-ups; particularly if they think they might give them an edge. On lakes and rivers that have not been heavily pressured they certainly can give you a big advantage, however, they're not the only option.

Carp are curious creatures and they will investigate anything they encounter that appears out of the ordinary, and what could be more out of the ordinary than a bit of food wafting around a couple of centimetres off the bottom? Carp are usually suckers for a pop-up during a lake's early fishing days but they also twig it pretty quickly too.

So when are the best times to use a pop-up presentation?

1. As an alternative presentation that catches for no other reason than it tickles the carp's curiosity.

2. To beat deep silt.

3. To present a bait over silkweed and other types of bottom weed.

## CURIOSITY
As was explained at the beginning of this chapter the initial reason the pop-up became so popular was simply because it offered a radically different alternative presentation. You'd think that no carp in its right mind would take a pop-up waving around a couple of inches off the bottom as it looks so unnatural...But take it they do, and sometimes for no other reason than it pushes their curiosity button. However, as we also pointed out earlier, it doesn't take carp long to twig the fact that such an unnatural looking bait spells danger so it has only a limited catching life.

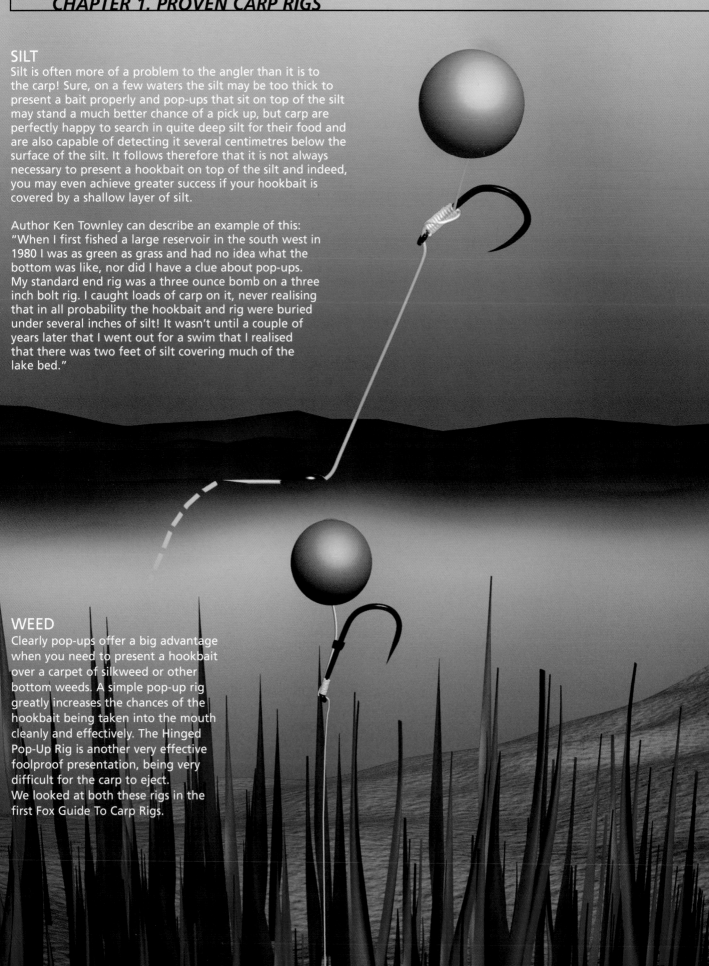

## SILT

Silt is often more of a problem to the angler than it is to the carp! Sure, on a few waters the silt may be too thick to present a bait properly and pop-ups that sit on top of the silt may stand a much better chance of a pick up, but carp are perfectly happy to search in quite deep silt for their food and are also capable of detecting it several centimetres below the surface of the silt. It follows therefore that it is not always necessary to present a hookbait on top of the silt and indeed, you may even achieve greater success if your hookbait is covered by a shallow layer of silt.

Author Ken Townley can describe an example of this: "When I first fished a large reservoir in the south west in 1980 I was as green as grass and had no idea what the bottom was like, nor did I have a clue about pop-ups. My standard end rig was a three ounce bomb on a three inch bolt rig. I caught loads of carp on it, never realising that in all probability the hookbait and rig were buried under several inches of silt! It wasn't until a couple of years later that I went out for a swim that I realised that there was two feet of silt covering much of the lake bed."

## WEED

Clearly pop-ups offer a big advantage when you need to present a hookbait over a carpet of silkweed or other bottom weeds. A simple pop-up rig greatly increases the chances of the hookbait being taken into the mouth cleanly and effectively. The Hinged Pop-Up Rig is another very effective foolproof presentation, being very difficult for the carp to eject. We looked at both these rigs in the first Fox Guide To Carp Rigs.

## Creating Pop-Ups

Normally pop-ups are fished between 2-4cm off the bottom and some type of weight is used to counter the buoyancy of the bait. Many pop-up presentations rely on critical or neutral buoyancy achieved by adding or removing tiny amounts of weight so the hookbait sinks very slowly. Here are a few methods of achieving this neutral buoyancy; whichever you choose, test, the presentation in the margins to ensure that all is well before casting out.

## HI-SG Tungsten Putty

An excellent alternative is the new ultra-heavy Fox Hi-SG Tungsten putty that allows for extremely delicate counter balancing. This can be moulded around swivels, rings or knots; you can even smear some putty along the length of the hook link itself to ensure that it lies hard on the lakebed rather than floating up off the bottom. If you wish to apply a big amount straight to the line first position a small float stop on the line, this gives the putty something to 'grip' when it is moulded around the stop and it is less likely to slip.

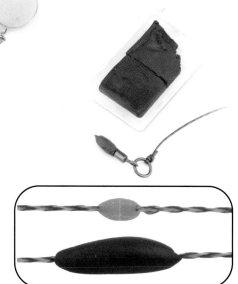

## Kwik Change Pop-Up Weights

While ordinary tungsten split shot works up to a point, better by far are our own Kwik Change Pop-Up Weights. This is due to their specially designed profile that cuts down on tangles considerably, and the fact they can be moved easily once they are on the line. In addition four sizes are available meaning the weight can be increased or decreased in an instant.

## 45lb Lead Core

Another method of critically balancing a pop-up is by using lead wire removed from the centre of 45lb Fox Leadcore. Hold the hook link tight by placing the hook in the butt ring and pulling on the link itself, tightly coil the lead wire four or five times around the material. Break off any excess then pinch the lead wire with a pair of pliers or forceps to make sure it stays in position. If need be you can position three or four of these little coils of lead wire throughout the length of the hook link so that it is pinned down hard to the lakebed.

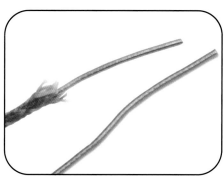

You can also add it to the hair immediately below the hookbait or you can even push it into the hookbait itself.

> *"There are a number of Pop-up presentations doing the rounds... but this one is very effective"*

There are any number of pop-up presentations doing the rounds at the moment but this one is very effective. As with most Pop-Up rigs, it tends to hook the carp in the lower lip, regardless of the direction the carp approaches the hookbait from.

You will need the following accessories:

- A size 6 Fox Arma-Point LSC
- Rubber Rig and Ring Stops
- Fox Rigidity in both 15lb and 25lb breaking strains
- Hi-SG Tungsten Putty
- 20lb Fox Pike Crimps and a pair of crimping pliers
- A size 7 and a size 11 Flexi Ring Swivel

**HI-SG RIG PUTTY**

**FOX RIGIDITY**

LENGTH
20m

B/S

STIFF RIG BRISTLE FILAMENT

DIAMETER - 0.41mm
SUPER RIGID
LOW VISIBILITY
STIFF RIG HOOKLINK

For more info visit
**www.foxint.com**

FOX is a Registered Trade Mark • Designed & Dev

## Here is how to tie the rig:

1. First position the two rubber stops and the rig ring on the shank of the hook.

2. Peel off a length of 25lb Rigidity and thread the end through the ring of the ringed swivel, then add a 20lb pike crimp...

3. ...before feeding the nylon through the eye of the hook. Now once again pass the same end through the ring and the crimp.

4. Using the crimping pliers compress the crimp to form a small loop of 25lb Rigidity at the eye of the hook, encompassing the trapped ring swivel.

5. Take a section of 15lb Rigidity and tie one end to the Flexi Ring Swivel at the hook and the other end to the ring in the size 7 Flexi Ring Swivel. The overall length of the Rigidity should be about 10cm.

6. Pack the Hi-SG around the size 11 swivel making sure not to impede the action of the ring.

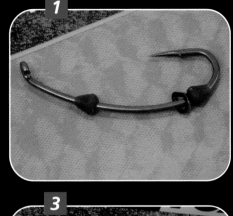

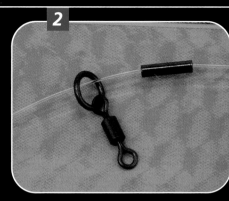

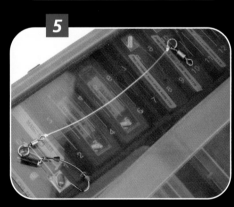

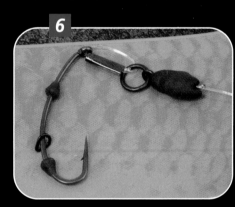

*Rig Ring*

*Size 6 Arma-Point LSC*

*Rubber Stops*

*Crimp*

*Hi-SG Tungsten Putty*

Finally, using the correct coloured bait floss tie the pop-up hookbait to the ring on the shank of the hook using the Knot-Within-A-Knot knot. Sequence shown in chapter 4.

Test the finished rig in the margins to make sure that the rig sinks quite quickly to the lakebed. This rig is not intended to be critically balanced and indeed it should be slightly over-weighted using the Hi-SG. In practice it is intended to hold tight to the bottom where it should sit upright off the lakebed.

When a carp approaches the hookbait the loop allows the hook to swivel towards the suction force applied by the fish to the hookbait, regardless of the angle of approach of the fish. Once inside the mouth the heavy counter weight falls down behind the lower lip, making the whole set-up very hard to eject without the hook pricking the lower lip.

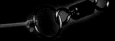

## CHAPTER 1. PROVEN CARP RIGS

Helicopter rigs have undergone a huge resurgence in popularity over the past few years. Although originally designed for distance fishing, the anti-tangle properties of the Helicopter rig make it suitable for most types of fishing.

The new Fox Helicopter Bead and Kit have been designed to be compatible with the new range of leads. Injection moulded in camo olive green, the low profile stem grips the lead loop and is long enough to accommodate a Speed Link and swivel, if used. The top bead provides a perfect shock absorber for the rig swivel and in conjunction with a dual bore Flexi Bead creates a tangle free rotary assembly.

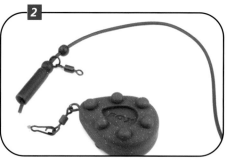

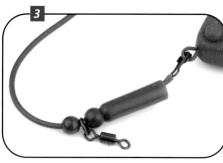

*1. Take your main reel line and thread on in the following order a) a section of anti-tangle tubing of the correct length (remember this needs to be about 10cm longer than the hooklink), b) the rubber shock bead, c) the Flexi Ring Swivel (line goes through the ring, NOT the swivel), and d) the specially designed beaded sleeve.*

*2. Tie on the Speed Link provided and attach a swivel lead of your chosen design and weight.*

*3. Slide the tubing down to the speed link passing it through the kit items as it goes.*

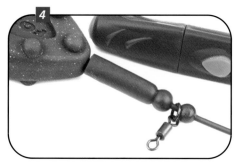

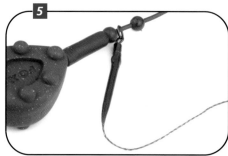

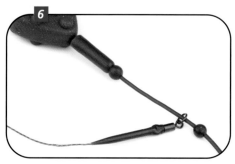

*4. Locate the beaded sleeve over the swivel and eye at the top of the lead and superglue the anti-tangle tubing into the sleeve.*

*5. That's the basic set-up and now all you need to do is attach the rig/hooklink of your choice to the eye of the swivel. We suggest that you use one of our new streamlined swivel sleeves to keep the end gear nice and tidy and ensure maximum anti tangle effect.*

*6. You will note that once wet the upper rubber shock bead slides very easily along the tubing so than in the event of a break or the fish being lost it can easily detach itself from the end gear.*

Much has been made over these past few years of the need to ensure that all leadcore set-ups are tied with the carp's welfare as a priority. Some fisheries have misguidedly banned the use of leadcore, claiming that it can damage fish. We would refute that, provided the set up is tied properly. Our helicopter accessories are totally carp friendly when used with both tubing and leadcore. Here is how to tie a safe leadcore helicopter rig using our Heli Kit. If you prefer, the Helicopter rigs shown on both these pages can be purchased assembled ready to go.

However, if using the kit here's how to set it up to its best advantage:

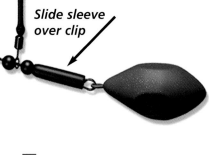

*Size 6 Fox Series 5*

*Slide sleeve over clip*

1. Take a section of 45lb Leadcore and having removed some of the inner core splice a small, neat eye at one end.

2 At the opposite end again remove some of the core then splice on the speed link.

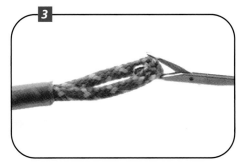

3. Cut a 5cm section of shrink tubing and thread it onto the leadcore using a baiting needle.

4. Slide the shrink tube down to the Speed Link then shrink it onto the leadcore in boiling water or over steam from a kettle.*

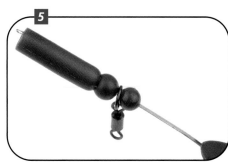

5. Onto a Lip-Close Baiting Needle thread, in the following order, a) the rubber shock bead, b) the flexi ring swivel (through the ring, NOT the swivel), and c) the specially designed bead and sleeve.

6. Locate the needle in the spliced loop at the end of the leadcore and transfer the contents of the needle onto the leadcore.

7. Slide the contents down so that they can be pushed over the shrink tube located next to the speed link.

8. Now all that remains is to attach your chosen hooklink and again we recommend that you use a swivel sleeve to keep the end gear nice and tidy.

* This operation should not be attempted by children under the age of 16 unless supervised by an adult.

## CHAPTER 1. PROVEN CARP RIGS

You may well have heard of the CV Safety Rig helicopter set up. This was designed many years ago by some of the very inventive guys fishing the Colne Valley. The CV rig was designed to create the safest possible helicopter set-up that was 100% safe in the event of a break as the component parts could easily disassemble and the fish would be left with only the hook and hooklink, which it could easily dispose of. Well you might be surprised that you can actually make a leadcore version of the CV Safety Rig!

As we constantly stress, it is very important to ensure that any rig that uses leadcore is totally carp friendly and we'll be the first to accept that it can cause problems if it is not used properly. One of the main problems associated with leadcore is the potential for the lead to jam against a loop or a stop or some other obstruction in the event of a break. In particular the helicopter rig and leadcore have always been uneasy bed-fellows as there is probably more potential for harm using a leadcore helicopter rig than any other, in inexperienced hands. While this rig may look complicated at first sight, it is easy to tie and is 100% safe.

While fishing, the rig acts as a bolt rig as the shock effect is produced by the way the hooklink is locked in place between the lead and the lower splice. However, in the event of a break behind the lead core, say at the mainline join or further along the mainline, what happens is this: The carp will pull the hooklink along the lead core against the weight of the lead. As it does so the swivel and the rubber bead slide along the lead core to the upper loop. Here the bead pulls free easily and the swivel falls free of any encumbrance. (Try it for yourself and see how well this system works.) The carp is now totally free of the mainline and the leadcore and all it has in its mouth is the hook and hooklink.

You will need the following: 45lb camo Leadcore; a splicing needle; three rubber rig beads; a Speed Link; Heli Kit; plus a rig and swivel lead of your choice.

*1. First take a section of lead core and splice a loop in each end.*

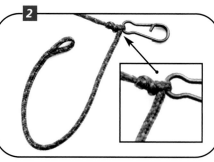

*2. Tie one end of the leadcore to the Speed Link using a 3-Turn Blood Knot. Make sure the knot does not trap the splice. You may think three turns is not enough, but with 45lb leadcore it is perfectly OK. Tighten the knot so that the rig looks like this.*

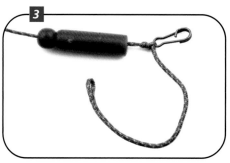

*3. Thread the bead and sleeve buffer onto the leadcore and slide it down towards the speed link.*

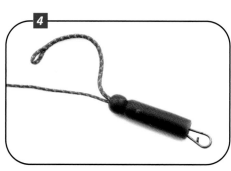

*4. Pull the other end of the lead core through the buffer using a baiting needle to look like this.*

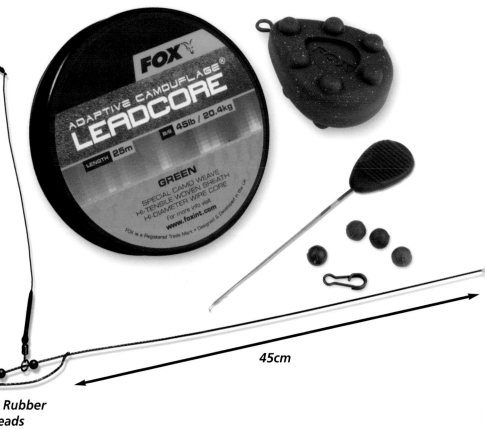

**Small Rubber Rig Beads**

45cm

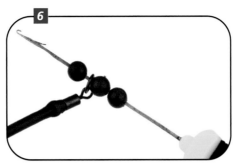

5. Now clip the lead to the speed link and push the bead and sleeve buffer over the speed link and the eye of the lead.

6. Thread the small rubber rig beads and the swivel of your hooklink onto a lip-close baiting needle exactly as shown.

7. Locate the lip of the baiting needle in the spliced loop at the opposite end of the lead core from the lead.

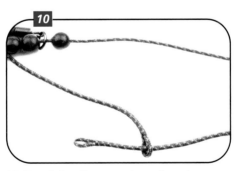

8. Slide the rig beads and the hooklink swivel over the splice and onto the leadcore. Remove the lip-close baiting needle.

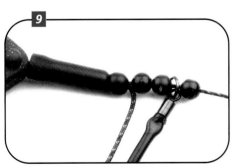

9. Run the beads and the hooklink swivel along the lead core and down to the lead weight that is clipped to the speed link.

10. Now bring the upper loop down to meet the lower one and pass one through the other.

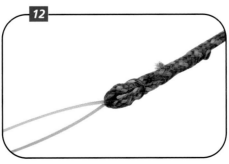

11. Straighten out the lead core. The rig will now look like this.

12. All that remains now is to attach the main line to the upper spliced-in loop using a loop to loop Knot.

## One handy tip:

If you are fishing over hard ground or on damaging gravel or stones remember that this type of lakebed can easily damage hook points and you may be required to change the hook and hooklink after each cast. We suggest that you substitute one of our Kwik Change Heli Swivels for the standard Flexi Ring swivel provided. Thus you can quickly and easily change hooklinks from the damaged one to a new pre-tied rig.

1. Locate the Kwik Change Swivel on the helicopter set-up as you would the normal swivel.

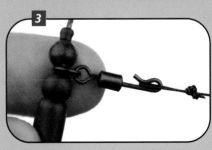

2. Tie a neat loop in the end of the rig and locate over the crook in the swivel.

3. Thread the sleeve up and over the Kwik Change Swivel to secure the hook length in place.

Here's a very effective leadcore helicopter rig that again uses a pop-up hookbait. It incorporates a very short hooklink and a pop-up hookbait that is fished directly off the leadcore. It is one of the most effective long range set-up going and is virtually 100% tangle-proof.

This ultra-short pop-up rig has become widely known as the Chod Rig. The rig is very effective, is based around a leadcore helicopter rig, and is one of the best long range set-ups going as it is virtually 100% tangle-proof. It incorporates a very short hook link and a pop-up hook bait that is fished directly off the leadcore. The rig looks a little strange but anyone who needs convincing of how effective it is should look at the 76lb 7oz caught by Fox consultant, Christian Finkelde, on the Chod Rig. Here's the story of how it was caught in Christian's own words:

"On Monday 24th October I packed my car and drove to my local lake of about 12 acres in size for an overnight session. The lake is quite difficult: it has a low stock, the fish are very pressured and the water is very rich in natural food. Nevertheless the lake was my target water for 2005.

I had caught a 44lb Common from the water the previous month but the swim I had caught the fish from in September had recently been unproductive, so I decided to try a new one that I hadn t fished before. During the summer I had spent quite a bit of time swimming and diving in the lake looking for features so I roughly knew what to expect in the new swim. Just to be on the safe side I plumbed the area with a few casts and found a nice little slope to my right.

I decided to fish one rod to my right at a distance of about 35 metres, and the second one to my left in a similar depth at about 25 metres. The water temperature had recently dropped quite a bit so I intended to fish in deep water.

My set up consisted of: 25lb Fox Submerge Plus braid as mainline, a two metre camo leadcore leader, a Chod Rig tied with 20lb Rigidity and a size 5 Fox Series 6 hook and a 6 oz Elevator lead. On one rod I fished with a 20mm Squid & Octopus Fluoro pop up from Dynamite Baits which I had cut into a cube. On the second one I used a 20mm Hi Attract Pineapple Plus pop up also from Dynamite Baits. I decided not to bait the swim and just fish a PVA bag on each rod. I opted for the new Fox / Mainline flavoured PVA bags and filled them with a mixture of Swim Stim green groundbait, 6mm Swim Stim pellets, 14mm Marine Halibut pellets and a bit of Pineapple Liquid from Dynamite Baits.

Once both rods were set up I cast them to their respective spots and set up the rest of my gear for the night. At 8.00 p.m. my good friend Patrick Scupin turned up for a chat. When Patrick left I read a book with my head torch, listened to the radio and went to bed early. At 6.20 a.m. I was awoken by a screaming take on my right hand rod (the one with the pineapple pop up).

After picking up the rod the fish straight away took line off my spool. It was still dark and the fish stayed deep and moved slowly. Step by step I pumped it closer but in between the fish took line several times. At that stage one thing was for sure if it wasn t a catfish on the other end of the line it must have been one of the big ones in the lake. It might sound strange but after about half of the fight my inner voice told me that this was the big common of the lake. In the margins the fish headed for a weed bed but with it being October the weed, fortunately, wasn t a dangerous snag anymore. In the moonlight I got the first glimpse of a big white spot on the water surface. My thoughts about the big common became more and more evident. Finally I managed to net the fish and there it was. The biggest common carp I ve ever seen. Incredible - all the hours of waiting for a take were forgotten. I carefully lifted the fish on the unhooking mat and unhooked it. I zeroed the scales and put the fish into the weigh sling making sure the fins were ok. With the aid of my Fox weighing handle I slowly lifted the fish. The needle of my scales first went past the 35 kg mark and then stopped at 34 kg 650 grammes (76lb and 7oz).

**1**

1. First take a 1.5m section of 45lb Camo Leadcore and at one end splice in a Speed Link and at the other splice a loop with a neat, small eye. The Speed Link will allow you to change the shape and weight of the lead according to conditions.

**2**

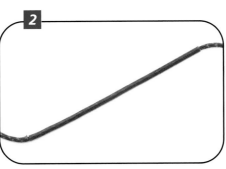

2. Now position a 3-4cm section of 1.2-0.4mm Fox Shrink Tube at the mid point of the leadcore and shrink it down in boiling water.

**3**

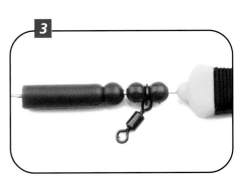

3. On a lip close baiting needle position the following: a Rubber Flexi Bead; a size 7 Flexi Ring Swivel; another rubber flexi bead; a Heli bead.

**4**

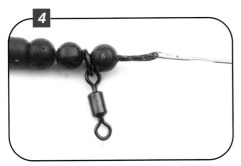

4. Transfer the contents of the needle to the leadcore by locating the crook of the needle in the spliced loop.

**5**

5. Clip the lead of your chosen design and weight to the Speed Link. Slide the Heli bead and sleeve down to cover and protect the leadcore in the area of the Speed Link and its attached lead.

**6**

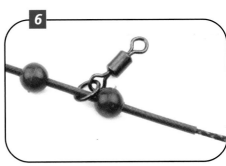

6. Position the beads and the ring swivel on the shrink tube. Note: it is the ring itself that goes onto the shrink tube, not the swivel.

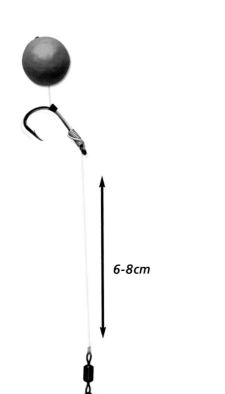

6-8cm

**7**

7. Now we need to tie the rig itself. Here we have used a simple knotless knot set up on a Fox Series 3 - size 4 hook using Fox 18lb Illusion Fluorocarbon.

**8**

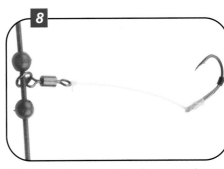

8. Tie the other end of the Illusion to the swivel located between the two beads on the shrink tube. The length of the hooklink should be about 6-8cm.

**9**

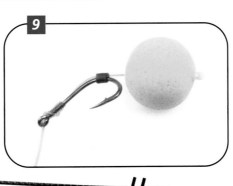

9. The rig is fished with a pop-up hookbait, the weight of the lead core being sufficient to pin the buoyant bait to the lakebed. The hookbait is fished directly off the lead core with no other counter weight.

150cm

* This operation should not be attempted by children under the age of 16 unless supervised by an adult.

## LEADCORE COMBI RIG

There is nothing new about combi rigs but you may well not have heard of the following set-up that uses leadcore to form the boom section of the combi rig. The result is a rig that casts like a dream without tangling and once on the lakebed the boom section lies tight to the bottom giving no cause for alarm from an approaching carp. The rig is best fished with a lightly buoyant hookbait that sits up off the lakebed, held down solely by the weight of the boom. The business section of the rig is a version of the Multi Rig, which was devised by Mike Kavanagh.

To tie the rig you will need:
• A length of 45lb Leadcore
• Two size 7 Flexi Ring Swivels
• A 2mm Rig Ring
• Size 6 Fox Arma-Point LSC hook
• A length of 30lb Armadillo in brown

# Here's how to tie the rig:

1. Strip a small section of leadcore and tie it to the ring in the first of the size 7 Flexi Ring Swivels.

2. Repeat the action so that you have a section of leadcore about 20cm long with a ringed swivel attached via the ring at each end.

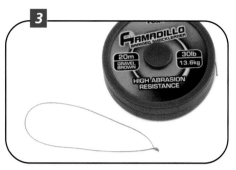

3. Take a six inch length of 30lb Armadillo and tie an overhand knot to join the two free ends together.

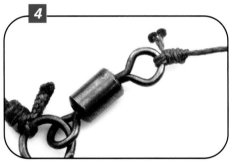

4. Pass this through the swivel of one of the Flexi Ring Swivels and form a three turn blood knot. Trim away the two joined ends.

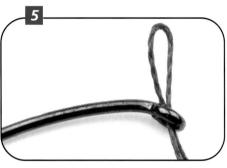

5. Pass the loop of braid up through the eye of the hook.

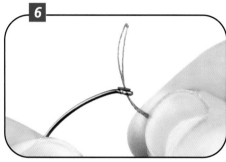

6. Thread the 2mm rig ring over the loop

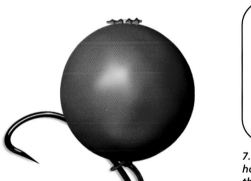

7. Now pass the loop over the point of the hook and position it on the shank opposite the point of the hook.

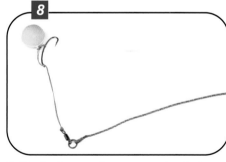

8. Finally, tie a small pop-up to the rig ring with bait floss. The lead core will hold it down without the need for extra weight.

The big advantage of this rig is its ultra stiff leadcore boom section coupled to a light and supple hook section. The small pop-up hookbait is held down by the weight of the boom section alone, so there is no need for tungsten putty. When a carp mouths the hookbait the supple section tends to turn and hold in the bottom lip, while the heavy boom section tends to draw the hook point downwards where it finds and initial hold on the lower lip.

6cm (Max)

Leadcore

20cm (Min)

# CHAPTER 2

## *Above The Lead*

In the first rig book we referred several times to what we call the End Zone. By this we mean not just the hook/hair arrangement but everything that falls within the last 2m of your end tackle: the lead and how it is attached to the hooklink material, the line behind the lead and so on. In this chapter we shall look in a bit more detail at the End Zone and also discuss ways of making your end tackle and indeed your main line as unobtrusive as possible.

As you may have gathered, leadcore is a firm favourite of the Fox Carp Team and if you read the last book you will have seen several presentations that used leadcore to good effect. In 2009 we upgraded our leadcore to make it denser and have improved the camouflage outer to help it blend in discreetly with the lakebed. In fact we have also taken into account the way the fibres in the outer weave change colour when wet. Some leadcore lines appear to be perfectly disguised to start with. However, when they have been in the water for a few minutes they darken creating a very obvious dark line leading to the lead and the hooklink. Even when soaked for many hours in the lake, our new Camo Leadcore retains a very obvious fleck, which breaks up its outline and helps it blend in with the surroundings.

You will also notice that our new leadcore is denser which ensures that the crucial section of line behind the lead is kept tightly pinned down to the lakebed. This prevents carp from coming into contact with the line behind the lead when it is approaching the hookbait. This is the most likely time for a cautious carp to suss that all is not well; if it comes into

contact with the line behind the lead it will almost certainly spook from the swim without touching your hookbait. Fox Camo Leadcore incorporates a hi-tensile woven outer sheath that is designed to withstand snags, heavy weed, pads and other abrasive underwater obstacles. It is also very effective as an anti tangle medium and lends itself perfectly to all the most up-to-date carp rigs. The new leadcore is perfect for subtle, unobtrusive presentations when fishing for wary, line-shy carp.

We have also made it available on bulk 25m spools for those anglers who like to use longer leadcore leaders, either when boating out baits or when fishing mega slack line set-ups at close range.

In addition, we also offer pre-tied versions including a standard ready-spliced length of 45lb leadcore with a size 7 Flexi Ring Swivel, a leadcore helicopter rig and a version that incorporates a lead safety clip and ringed swivel.

*"Ready made leadcore leaders are available with Heli Beads, Flexi Ring Swivels, Safety Lead Clips and Safety Sleeves attached"*

*"Leadcore ensures carp don't come into contact with the line and spook when approaching the hook bait"*

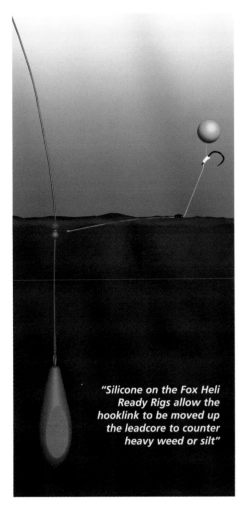

*"Silicone on the Fox Heli Ready Rigs allow the hooklink to be moved up the leadcore to counter heavy weed or silt"*

Each helicopter rig is spliced at each end and glued for extra security. The spliced loop ensures quick and easy attachment to the mainline while the speed link allows the angler to quickly change the lead size and shape without breaking down the rig. They are also fitted with the new unique Fox Heli Bead and a sliding silicone stop. The rig is therefore adjustable to allow the hooklink to be moved along the leadcore to the position of the angler's choice to counter heavy weed or thick silt.

Similarly the version that incorporates a lead clip is also pre-spliced and glued and comes to you with the safety lead clip already attached to the flexi ring swivel. All you need to do is attach the rig and hooklink of your choice and attach the mainline to the pre-spliced loop at the other end of the leadcore. What could be simpler?

Though we wax lyrical about leadcore we have to accept that there are some anglers who don't like (or are not allowed) to use leadcore behind the lead. However, it is still important to disguise the line behind the lead as effectively as possible so we have come up with a very dense tungsten tube that hugs the lakebed even better than leadcore.

The new Loaded Tungsten Rig Tube is exclusive to Fox and it is impregnated with a high percentage of tungsten granules. This creates a rig tube that is extremely dense and significantly heavier than any other tubing currently available. This tubing is also easy to thread, even when wet, and will accommodate main lines up to 20lb breaking strain. In addition it provides fantastic protection for the mainline in that crucial area behind the lead where damage is most likely to occur.

As with leadcore, the new tubing is designed to keep the terminal tackle tight on the bottom where it is less likely to spook a wary carp.

Continuing with our theme of concealing as much of the endzone behind the lead as possible, we should not move on until we have considered the usefulness of backleads in all their guises including flying, captive and clip-on. Although the endzone is the most critical area to "pin down", keeping the line between the end zone and the rod tip close to the lake provides lots of advantages. Roaming carp are less likely to inadvertently swim into the line and bolt which helps to distinguish between line bites and the reel thing.

Fox Sliders are a type of flying back lead that have been specially designed with a wind resistant face that catches the wind and forces the little pin down lead up the line on the cast.

It has to be said that Sliders are not ideally suited for every type of lakebed. We will look at where not to use them shortly. However, in certain circumstances they are an invaluable aid; keeping your main line down on the deck, where it cannot spook feeding carp. Such a situation could be when you are fishing a reasonably flat lakebed with not too many pronounced contours such as bars, plateaux and gullies. You may think that there are not too many lakes like this but many reservoirs, sand workings and estate lakes are characterised by their lack of underwater features and on these kinds of waters the Sliders really come into their own. Conversely, if you mainly fish gravel pits, with their associated bars, gullies and plateaux, then their usefulness may possibly be less obvious.

In a moment we'll look at a few angling situations and assess how Sliders can help you, but first a brief word about carp care when using these flying pin down leads. Though the central bore of the Sliders is comparatively large, it is impossible to make the hole so large that it would pass over any knot in the set up as that would defeat the object of the wind catching properties of the back lead. The idea is for them to catch the wind and the resistance forces them back up the mainline towards the caster. Were the hole to be any larger, the air resistance would be reduced and the lead would not fly up the line properly. That being the case it is important to ensure that the comparatively small central hole in the Slider can pass unhindered over any knots in the set up such as shock leader and abrasion resistant leader knots.

*The knot produced here attaching 30lb Slink to 10lb mono is to large for the Slider to pass over"*

*Knotting 10lb mono to a Tapered Leader produces a more streamlined knot the slider can pass over"*

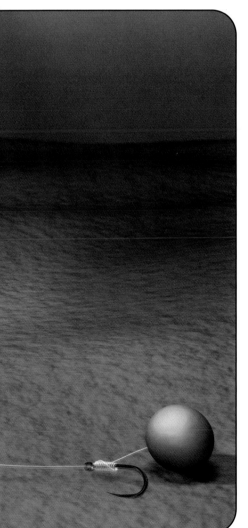

In an ideal world it would be preferable to have no knots behind the Slider at all, but it must be acknowledged that there will be times - when casting long distances or fishing at range for instance - when you will need to use a stronger nylon or braided shock leader such as 45lb Armadillo, 20lb Soft Steel or one of our tapered Soft Steel shock leaders.

In practice you will find that the last two, when knotted to 10lb main line with the proper knot (such as the Albright Knot which we cover later in the book), will produce a shock leader knot that the Slider can pass over unhindered. However, in the case of the former two, the leader knot is generally too bulky to allow a Slider to pass easily. Before you cast out the rig it is always best to test whether the Slider will not hang up on the leader knot and if you are in any doubt do not use a Slider.

Take a look at the image on the left. This shows a fairly flat, gently sloping lakebed with few exaggerated contours. In such a situation a Slider is highly recommended. As you can see, it has forced the main line to lie snugly out of the way along the bottom and thus well out of the way of any carp in the vicinity. Don't forget, carp can detect your mainline by both sight and feel and so it is imperative to keep as much line close to the bottom as possible if you are fishing for spooky fish that are heavily pressured.

We also advise that you use a 0.75-1.00m length of leadcore behind the main lead in order to reduce the spook factor still further. Place the Slider on your main line, before tying it to the leadcore. That way it will be free to fly up the line on the cast.

If you don't want the Slider to fly too far back towards you on the cast you can limit the distance it travels by tying a simple well trimmed knot of PVA tape at the point on the main line where you want the Slider to end up. In a few moments the PVA will melt and the Slider will be free to move up and down the main line and will not pose a safety threat in the event of a break. The best knot to use for this is the Uni Knot shown on the right.

## Uni Knot

The Uni Knot is ideal for placing a stop or reference point on the main-line without weakening it. It has many uses: when tied with Magic Marker, it can be used as a reference point for distance; and in the example on this page we use PVA to form a stop knot.

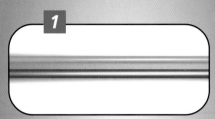

*"Take the shorter length of line and lay it along the main line".*

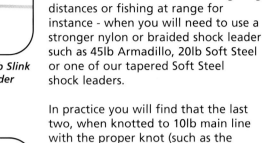

*"Take one end back on itself to form a loop".*

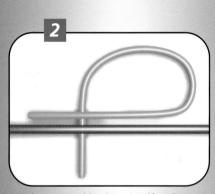

*"Take the tag end back through the loop four times".*

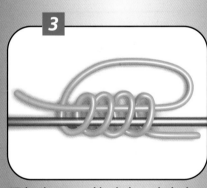

*"Moisten the knot with saliva as you pull it tight. Once the knot has been formed, with gentle pressure the knot can be moved along the line".*

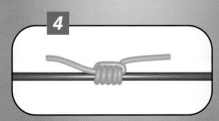

## CHAPTER 2. ABOVE THE LEAD

In this diagram you will note the presence of weed lying close to the lakebed between you and your target casting area. Don't be put off using a Slider in such a situation. As you can see, even though on this particular cast the Slider has landed between you and the weed bed, with the End Zone lying some distance away on the other side of the weed, you will also note that the main line remains much closer to the lakebed than would be the case were you fishing tight to the lead. True, there is a chance that a patrolling fish may be able to detect the main line slightly more readily but any attempt to sink the main line close to the bottom is better than none. In such a situation you would be well advised to increase the length of the leadcore behind the lead to about 1.5m.

Unfortunately weed comes in different densities and thicknesses and in some cases a Slider may be more trouble than it is worth. It is therefore advisable to do your homework with the marker float first before considering using a Slider. If you have only sparse bottom weed, then all well and good. However, if the weed grows from lakebed to surface then clearly a Slider is going to hinder not help.

We now come to a situation where a Slider will be less useful. In this diagram below, we are fishing a typical gravel pit and you can see that the Slider has landed between two bars with your hookbait landing in the gully behind the second bar, an area that you have discovered is a patrol route. The main line lies across the top of the bar with the line going down tight to the lead on the far side.

The Slider sits in the gully between the first and second bars, possibly suspended between the two and not actually on the lakebed at all. Not only will this spook any carp patrolling the first gully, it will also tend to increase the abrasion on the main line where it passes over the second bar. In the event of a run, the weakened line could cause you to get shredded off on the take.

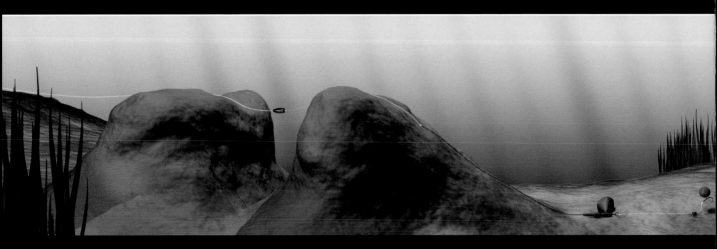

In situations where there is heavy weed
growth or lots of snags it can be a good
idea to fish with the rod tips high in the
air. This protects the line and maintains
direct contact with the lead - fishing in
this manner is particularly effective
for long range work on big
european venues.

## CHAPTER 2. ABOVE THE LEAD

Many anglers dismiss back leads, saying they decrease sensitivity. While this may be true to a certain extent, there are times when their advantages greatly outweigh their disadvantages. For instance, backleads greatly reduce the effect of a strong cross wind that can cause an excessive bow in the line and they are also useful for defeating surface scum or drifting weed. One of their main advantages is in keeping your other lines from getting in the way when playing a hooked fish. Also where there is an abundance of wild life a back lead can help keep the lines out of the bird's way!

There are two types of margin back lead, captive and clip-on. The Captive Back Leads come in four sizes: 35gm, 60gm, 85gm and 112gm. For long range fishing or use on rivers or lakes with a lot of tow, the larger sizes come into there own. Conversely, for smaller lakes and shorter range choose a lighter size.

The Captive Backleads are simple to use: after you cast out, the backlead is attached to the main line via a line gate mechanism similar to those found on the Fox Butt Swingers. You then allow the lead to slide down the line to the lakebed below the rod tips.

But here's the clever part: the back lead is in turn attached to a length of bright yellow fluorescent cord that is wound around a specially designed holder. As the lead slips down your main line you pay out the cord as well. When the back lead hits the lakebed simply slip the cord into one of the two securing slots on the holder. When a take occurs the little clip on the back lead springs open on the strike and the back lead drops into the margins at your feet. This is preferable in most cases to the alternative where a clip-on back lead remains on the line throughout the fight.

You can even attach the Captive Back lead in such a way that it releases the line on the run rather than on the strike. By positioning the back lead so that a severe angle is produced under the rod tip, and then securing it tightly via the securing cord, the take itself is usually enough to open the gate and allow the line to fly off the reel.

Quite often it is a good tactic to use both Sliders and Captive back leads together, if the circumstance and conditions allow. The more you can keep your line out of the way and out of view, the better.

*Fox Captive Back Leads are attached to a bar, which in turn is clipped to your rod pod. There are Backlead Bars available for most Fox rod pod systems.*

*"Open the line gate mechanism on the back lead".*

*"Place the main line in the gap on the lead".*

*"Close the line gate mechanism securing the main line in place".*

*"Feed the back lead down in to the margins then secure the coloured nylon in the slot on the winder".*

Clip-on back leads are attached to the main line after you have cast out and are allowed to sink to the lake bed. When a take occurs they slide down the line during the fight and end up resting against the casting lead. Opinions are divided about their effectiveness but as with Sliders, in the right situation there are second to none. Unlike Captive Backleads, the best rule of thumb is to use the lightest model you can get away with.

The Fox Down Rigger backleads have an ergonomic, moulded clip that allows single handed attachment to the line. This removes the problems associated with trying to hold the rod, line and backlead all at once. The clip itself is moulded from a low friction material allowing the lead to slide down either braided or mono mainlines. This helps both with positioning the backlead and when playing a hooked fish. In the event of it becoming trapped in weed or snags, it will pull free, putting the angler back in direct contact with the fish.

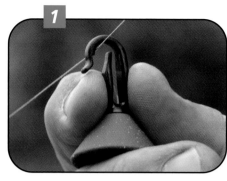

*"A special clip allows the Down Rigger backlead to be attached to the line with a single hand".*

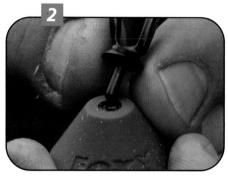

*"If the backlead gets snagged, the two parts separate under light pressure".*

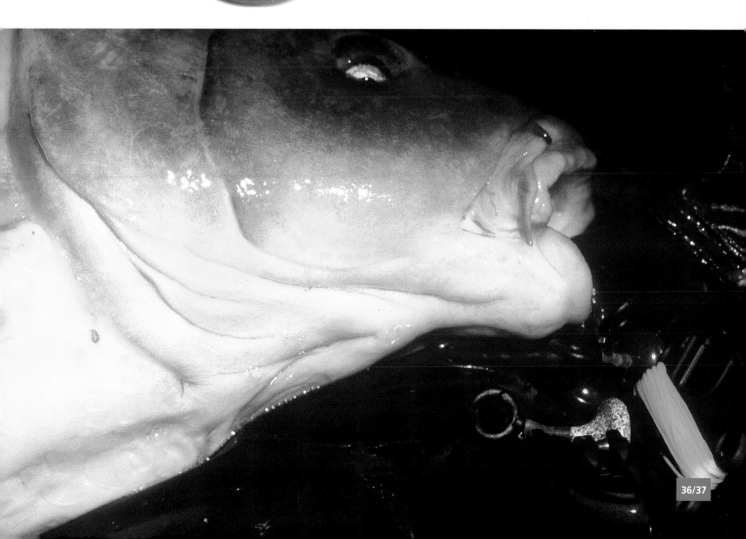

## CHAPTER 2. ABOVE THE LEAD

No chapter on concealment above the lead would be complete without a look at fluorocarbon mainlines and the part they can play in disguising this vital area. Fluorocarbon exhibits the lowest sub-surface visibility of any monofilament, with a Light Refraction Index of just 1.42 (only 0.09 different from that of water). Standard monofilaments tend to fall somewhere between 1.53 and 1.62 making them far more obtrusive to wary fish.

Fluorocarbons do tend to be slightly stiffer than the equivalent diameter monofilament and this inherent stiffness means if you are casting long distances copolymer monofilaments such as Soft Steel may be a better choice. However, the new Illusion XS has certainly bridged the casting gap between monofilament and fluorocarbon.

One of the biggest advantages of our Illusion fluorocarbon is that it is 78% denser than water whereas standard monofilaments are just 15% denser than water. This results in Illusion sinking extremely quickly where normal monofilaments can seem almost neutrally buoyant at times. Many of the Fox Carp Team have been using the new Illusion XS to great effect since its release in late-2009 and they all believe

it has put several fish on the bank that may not otherwise have been fooled. When fluorocarbons are used in conjunction with a length of leadcore or tungsten tube behind the lead, and Slider up the line it probably represents the ultimate in disguise. The whole of your main line, from rod tip to lead is concealed and there is nothing there for the carp to get suspicious of!

However, to obtain the maximum benefit of fluorocarbon you must fish with a slack line so it can take up the contours of the bottom.

Slack line fishing is something that many anglers do not feel confident about doing, but it is one of the best ways of fooling cautious carp. Can we suggest that you at least give the following set up a try? Hopefully it will give you confidence to use the method on more waters and will almost certainly lead to more fish on the bank.

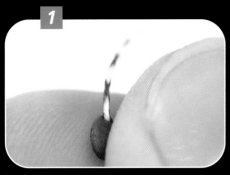

1. Add 'mouse droppings' of Hi-SG Tungsten putty at intervals along the hooklink to ensure it too remains pinned down to the lakebed.

2. Adjust your bankside set up so that the rear rests are higher than the top of the buzzers. This will mean that the rod tips point down towards the surface.

3. Cast out to your baited area and gently tighten up, taking care not to move the Slider along the line nearer to the lead.

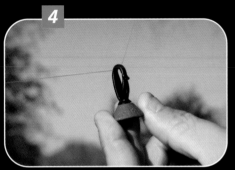

4. Attach a margin back lead (bearing in mind what may be lying between you and your hookbait as outlined earlier).

5. Place the rod in the rests and attach the indicator.

6. Now pay off line from the reel until the indicator hangs slackly down.

7. After a few minutes you will note that tension will have returned to the line and the indicators may have lifted a bit so peel off more line. Allow the line to settle so that it rests on the lakebed, following the contours of any underwater features.

8. Wait a few minutes more then lift the indicator up to the rod then allow it to fall under it own weight. You may need to do this several times. This will take some of the slack in the set up but not enough to lift the line off the bottom.

9. Now very carefully retrieve line a centimetre at a time by turning the spool of the reel (not the handle) until the indicator just starts to show a tiny amount of tension. It is advisable to use the lightest bobbins you can get away with when slack line fishing. The set up is now fine tuned so that you will get an immediate indication of a take, even as the line is starting to lift off the bottom as the run develops.

S lack line fishing requires a bit of a leap of faith as often it is quite far removed from what you may be accustomed to. Remember, the density of the Illusion main line means the line will be taking up the contours of the lake bed and by using this in conjunction with the long length of leadcore and a Slider flying back lead, the spook factor is virtually zero.

We reckon that disguising the End Zone and the rest of your gear between the rod and the lead is equally as vital as using a good bait and an efficient rig. In this day and age, when carp are under ever increasing pressure, any advantage you can get will pay dividends. The steps outlined here will help you keep your End Zone and main line out of the way from passing or feeding carp which will greatly improve your chances.

*"Fluorocarbon is denser than water which means it sinks when submerged"*

## *CHAPTER 2. ABOVE THE LEAD*

Of course, all this concealment is to no avail unless you are using a rig and End Zone set up that produces an immediate bolt effect. So before we close this chapter let's just have a look at one of the discoveries of 2005, the 360 Degree Rig.

This rig has been largely attributed to Dave Lane. One thing's for sure; whoever thought it up did the carp world a favour as this rig represents a considerable step forward in rig technicalities.

One of the most important items of tackle used in the construction of this rig are the new Rubber Rig and Ring Stops.

These have been designed to create the ultimate in modern anti-eject rigs as they feature injection moulded stops with a unique shape that act as a buffer for the rig ring without being overly bulky on the hook shank. These are an integral part of the 360 Degree Rig.

To tie the rig you will need the following: A pair of rubber rig stops and a rig ring from the above, a size 6 Fox Arma-Point LSC hook, a size 11 and size 7 Flexi Ring swivel, a coated hooklink material and lead weight of your choice.

We'll go over its construction step-by-step:

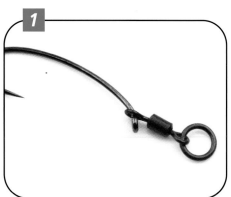

*1. First slip the eye of the size 11 Flexi Ring swivel onto the hook shank like this.*

*2. Now add the first of the Rubber rig stops and position it close to the eye so it keeps the Flexi Ring swivel in place close to the eye. Ensure that the stop does not actually prevent the hook from rotating within the swivel, while at the same time maintaining its position close to the eye of the hook.*

*3. Slip a small rig ring onto the shank... Followed by the second moulded stop. (Note that the bulbous part of the stops should face inwards to prevent the ring from passing over).*

*4. You are going to need a coated hooklink material as this rig works best when fished combi rig fashion. Fox Cortex is ideal.*

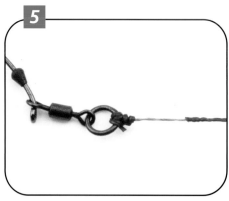

*5. The rig seems to work best when fished on longer than average hooklinks, say 30cm or so. First cut off the required amount of hooklink material and strip away a small section of outer coating before attaching to the ring in the Flexi Ring swivel.*

*6. Attach the other end of the hooklink to the ring in the size 7 flexi ring swivel, tie your mainline/leadcore to the swivel part and attach your lead. Here we are using a Kling On in-line lead.*

*1.5 - 2cm*

*25lb Insider*

*Peeled Section*

*25 - 30cm*

Once you have completed the rig you need to attach the hookbait. Bait selection is vital for 360 rig to work effectively. You want to chose a small lightly buoyant hookbait as the 360 Degree Rig works much better when it is not counter weighted in any way whatsoever. In other words all that is required to take the hookbait slowly down to the lakebed is the weight of the hook and the swivel.

*"Hook bait selection is vital for 360 rig to work effectively"*

The best way to attach the bait to the rig is by tying it with bait floss to the rig ring that runs freely along the shank. Fox now produce Bait Floss in five different colours to match different baits, so select the colour which matches your bait. We use a special knot to tie the hookbait to the rig ring. It is called the Knot-Within-A-Knot Knot. Full step-by-step instructions covering this knot appear in Chapter 4.

Attaching the bait in this manner means it maintains more of its watertight integrity so it stays buoyant for longer. It also maintains its flavour and smell for longer too.

Finally test the rig in the edge to ensure that it sinks. If it remains on the surface chose a smaller pop-up. Alternatively, although not ideal, you can mould some Hi-SG Tungsten Putty around the barrel of the mini ringed flexi swivel, taking care not to impede the action of the swivel.

*This rig has been largely attributed to Dave Lane*

40/41

# CHAPTER 3

*Bite Detection*

# FOX GUIDE TO MODERN CARP FISHING

## CHAPTER 3. BITE DETECTION

In the last chapter we looked at ways of increasing sensitivity at the business end of your set up, so now we need to consider how to make the actual detection of bites more sensitive. We touched briefly on this in the first book but now it's time to go into the subject in a little more detail. There are several ways in which you can improve bite detection and without a doubt one of the most positive ways is to switch to braided main line such as Gravitron Pro. The members of the Fox Carp Team are all huge fans of braided line and all will tell you that the increased sensitivity has to be experienced to be believed.

So what exactly is braided reel line? Most of you will have heard about braided hooklink materials and braided abrasion resistant leaders like Armadillo? Well, braided reel line is rather similar.

All braids serve a specific purpose and should not be used out of context. Here we are dealing purely with braids that have been designed solely as reel lines; not as hooklinks, shock leaders or abrasion leaders. You may hear all kinds of scare stories concerning braids but don't believe all you hear.

For instance: People will tell you that the chance of a hook pull is increased if you are using braid, due to the total lack of stretch in the line. This is simply not true! Ask anyone who has been using braid for some time if they loose more fish under the tip than they did when using nylon and they will say, not at all.

OK, if you are too heavy handed with a fish and bully it too much then there is perhaps a slightly bigger chance of a hook pull. But the answer is simple and fish-friendly, namely, don't bully them in the first place and all will be fine.

Set the clutch a little bit lighter than you would if you were using nylon and you should have no problems whatsoever. In addition we think you'll find you enjoy the fight that much more, as every tug, pull and surge of power from the fish is transmitted down the stretch-free braid, through the rod and right into your fingertips.

It's a brilliant sensation and you'll never realise how much you miss when you play a fish on nylon!

You may hear that braid is prone to tangling and that wind knots cause problems. Used properly you should never suffer from bird's nests or tangles and provided you close the bale arm correctly wind knots will not be a problem. Two points to remember: First, don't build the line up right to the edge of the spool as you would with nylon. If you do then tangles are more likely to occur. Second, when you put the bale arm over after casting make sure you do so on a tight line. If the braid is slack as the bale arm goes over the potential for a wind knot is increased.

Another often quoted criticism of braided main lines is that the line can bed down too tightly on the spool during a fight or when retrieving heavy leads from extreme distance, which in turn hampers casting performance. This can occur with some flat profile braids, however our Gravitron Pro has a round profile which prevents excessive bedding in.

Loading braid onto the reel isn't simply a case of tying it to the spool and winding away. If the braid is loaded straight onto the reel, there is a chance the mass of braid can move on the spool when the clutch is fully engaged - even on plastic or non alloy spools. There are a number of solutions to prevent this. The easiest method is to wind a thin layer of electrical tape around the spool to give the braid something to grip against. However, the method we would suggest, which is shown on the opposite page, has a number of distinct advantages: Firstly, the nylon provides a far more secure surface for the braid to bed against; secondly, braid is more expensive than monofilament and has a smaller diameter for any given breaking strain. Therefore, loading braid on to a deep spool can be a costly business. Using nylon backing reduces the amount of braid that is needed to fill the spool.

GV SINKING BRAID GRAVITRON PRO DARK GREEN 20lb / 9.1kg Ø 0.35mm 600m
- Low Diameter Sinking Braid
- Low Vis Matt Olive Green
- Ultra Supple
- Abrasion Resistant
- Available in 300m & 600m
FOX is a Registered Trade Mark Designed & Developed in the UK For more info visit www.foxint.com FOX

To load the braid you will need: a bucket of water; rod butt section; budget priced monofilament; braid blades and the braid itself.

1. Thread the line through the butt ring of the rod.

2. Using a blood knot form a loop before tightening the monofilament to the spool.

3. Place the spool of line in a bucket of water then wind the line through the thumb and forefinger. Doing this reduces line twist considerably.

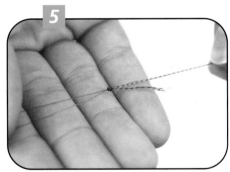

4. It's very difficult to judge exactly how much nylon backing is needed on any spool. In this instance, we have filled the spool to just over half way with nylon. This will require approximately 250 metres of braid to fill the spool.

5. Using back to back blood knots join the braid to the monofilament.

6. Place the spool of braid back in the water then continue to fill the spool, ensuring that the joining knot is placed right at the base of the spool, out of the way.

8. When making the first few casts with braid it is sensible to carefully bed the line down by making a few short, gentle casts first, followed by gradually increasing distances. The line should be retrieved with the rod tip beneath the surface and under tension – this ensures the braid is wound back onto the spool tightly and is nice and wet too. Never, under any circumstances arrive at your chosen venue with reels containing freshly loaded braid, and go for a big chuck straight away – accidents will happen which can prove expensive!

7. The finished result should look like this, with the braid coming to within a few of millimetres of the lip of the spool. A spool which is not filled this far reduces potential casting distances substantially. By the same token, over filling past this point can result in wind knots when casting.

# "The increased sensitivity has to be experienced to be believed"

People will tell you that braid damages fish. There's no getting away from the fact that if you use braid right through to the lead then the potential for damage is valid. However, use a 1m length of leadcore or a similar length of tungsten tubing behind the lead and the likelihood of damaging the fish is no greater than if you were using nylon.

It can be tricky feeding braided line such as Gravitron Pro through tubing but the job is made simple if you use a pole elastic threader from the Fox Match range. Simply push the wire threader through the tubing, thread the end of your Gravitron Pro through the loop at the end of the threader and pull it through. Job done!

Some anglers claim that braid does not cast as far as nylon. True, it takes a bit of getting used to but once you have got the hang of casting with braid you'll find you will actually increase the distance you can cast rather than reduce it.

Casting in a strong cross wind is never easy but the thinner diameter of braid means it is doesn't catch the wind and 'belly' as much as nylon. No doubt all of you who use nylon reel lines must know how frustrating it can be when you are faced with a big side wind. You watch the lead fly out and even see it splash down, but you'll never be able to feel it down onto the lake bed due to the belly in the line, and the stretch and general insensitivity of the nylon. With braid, the lack of stretch means you will still be able to feel the lead down to the bottom.

We need to stress one important safety factor about braided main line particularly when casting. Remember that braid is much finer than nylon line of the same breaking strain – 25lb Gravitron Pro is about the same as 8lb nylon – and this coupled with the total lack of stretch can cause quite serious injury to your index (casting) finger unless you take the following precautions.

First, always tighten the clutch fully before casting out. If the clutch can slip on the power stroke of the cast, the braid will cut into your index finger like a knife and may even cut right through to the bone in extreme cases. Obviously this is far less of a problem when using nylon (though it can occur) but you should be aware of the risk when using braided reel line.

MONOFILAMENT

BRAID

CROSS WIND

## Mahin Knot

*The Mahin Knot is an excellent knot for joining a leader to the mainline.*

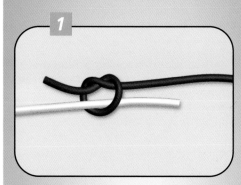

*"Tie a simple overhand knot in the mainline and thread the leader material through it".*

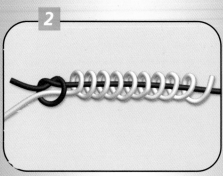

*"Wrap the leader around the leader 10 times working away from the overhand knot".*

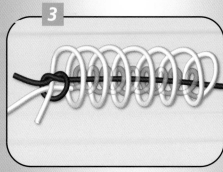

*"Form another eight loops over the top of the previous ones then pass the tag end back through the loop in the main line".*

*"Moisten the knot with saliva as you pull it tight. The finished knot should be neat and compact".*

To be on the safe side, always use some form of protection on your index finger. A leather finger stall can be obtained from your local chemist and it only costs a couple of quid. Alternatively spend a bit more and buy a soft leather golf glove.

Some anglers like to use a nylon shock leader to provide a bit of stretch at the business end. This eliminates the possibility of the casting injury that we have just discussed. It also provides a cushioning effect when the fish is under the tip, a buffer of nylon line to absorb the carp's power surges during the last few critical minutes of the fight. Bear in mind however, that the more stretchy nylon leader may actually reduce the power you are capable of generating on the cast and distance may be reduced.

There are several purpose designed nylon shock leaders available and Fox Amradillo in 30lb breaking strain takes some beating. However, for the ultimate in casting performance and smoothness you won't beat a specially designed tapered casting leader. Fox offer two breaking strains; 12-35lb and 15-45lb. To attach the leader to the braid we can thoroughly recommend the Mahin Knot. This is illustrated on the right and is also featured in the Fox Guide to Millennium Carping DVD's.

## CHAPTER 3. BITE DETECTION

Many anglers seem to think that braided line only really comes into its own when used for long range fishing, however, it has loads of advantages when fishing at short range and even for margin fishing. You should be aware that takes are usually blistering and you cannot just pick up the rod and hit the run as the lack of stretch in the line could well cause a hook pull or even a break. However, if you stay cool and don't get yourself into a panic you won't have any problems in this respect.

One very clear advantage of using braid is the way it takes up the contours of the lakebed. No matter how supple your nylon line it is unlikely it will be able to settle on the bottom in such an inconspicuous manner as braid. Braid blends into the lakebed better and reduces the risk of the carp detecting the line. It also reduces the possibility of line bites.

When close range or margin fishing we again suggest a long section of our Camo leadcore behind the lead, perhaps as long as 2m if you can get away with it. This helps to reduce still further the possibility of the carp coming into contact with the line behind the lead. The leadcore also protects the fish from any possible damage that might occur when the braid under tension comes into contact with the carp's flank and dorsal fin during a fight.

All the above are important considerations when it comes to making the decision to move over to braid but the main and significant advantage it has over nylon is its sensitivity. Even if you are fishing the big foreign reservoirs at ranges of 200m or more, the slightest movement of the lead will give a visual indication and an audible one. Usually the indicator lifts and you get several bleeps from the buzzer.

If you are using nylon line on a hard-pressured water where you think fish are capable of ejecting a hookbait with no visual or audible indication whatsoever, try switching to braid and see the difference. A carp only needs to breath on the hookbait and you know about it!

Sensitivity is the keyword with braid. You can always tell when a carp picks up the bait, whereas in many situations you'd most probably never even get a bleep if you were on nylon. In some situations this can allow the angler to react to subtle occurrences, occasionally resulting in a bonus fish.

*"Italian Fox consultant, Sandro Di Cesare, with a 30kg plus carp taken on braid"*

Let's just round off this section by going over the advantages of braid:

1. You make instant contact with the fish on the strike.

2. In hit and hold situations the lack of stretch prevents a hooked fish from getting into the snags or burying itself too deeply in weed.

3. 25lb braid has around the same diameter as 8lb mono. This gives extra casting range and also greater power when dealing with snaggy or weedy situations.

4. Braids last far longer than nylon lines.

5. There are no "memory" problems with braid. Some nylon lines are prone to spring off the reel in tangling coils.

6. Braided lines do not cause any more damage to a hooked fish during the scrap than nylon ones, provided you pay attention to the safety tips we mentioned earlier.

7. You can use braided main line for all types of fishing situations and it can actually improve your ratio of takes to fish landed due to its increased sensitivity and lack of stretch.

8. Many of the modern braids such as Gravitron Pro use a blend of Dyneema (one of the strongest known materials) and hi-tensile materials that have a very high Specific Gravity. This means the braids are not only extremely strong and low in diameter, but once they have cut through the surface film they will sink very quickly and hug the contours of the lakebed.

9. The thrill of fighting a powerful carp is a real mind-blowing experience as the lack of stretch means that every lunge, twist and turn is felt at the rod much more positively. This is a big advantage as it helps you feel the way a fish is fighting much better and you can tell more easily which way it is heading. It is really heart stopping to feel a big fish lunge on the end of your line, especially when fishing at extreme range way out in the middle of the lake. If you were using nylon under such circumstances you would feel just a steady, heavy weight whereas with braid you are locked in savage combat with the fish right from the word go. Once you've become accustomed to the feel of fighting a carp on braid you will really enjoy the sensation and will never go back to nylon!

Of course, there are other ways of increasing sensitivity at the rods and clearly the most obvious is to turn the sensitivity setting on your buzzers to maximum. All of our Micron Bite Alarms (with the exception of the N, M+ and MX+ models), feature adjustable sensitivity control, in some cases featuring no less than 8 sensitivity settings. Clearly, where conditions allow, the sensitivity control should be set at it highest setting.

Line clips too greatly aid bite detection by creating a more sensitive line angle at the buzzer. Attach the clip so that when the rod is placed to your liking on the pod the clip is positioned on the butt section only as far back from the alarm head as the length of the arm of your bite indicator. This has the effect of greatly increasing the sensitivity of the set up and both visual and audible indication is much improved.

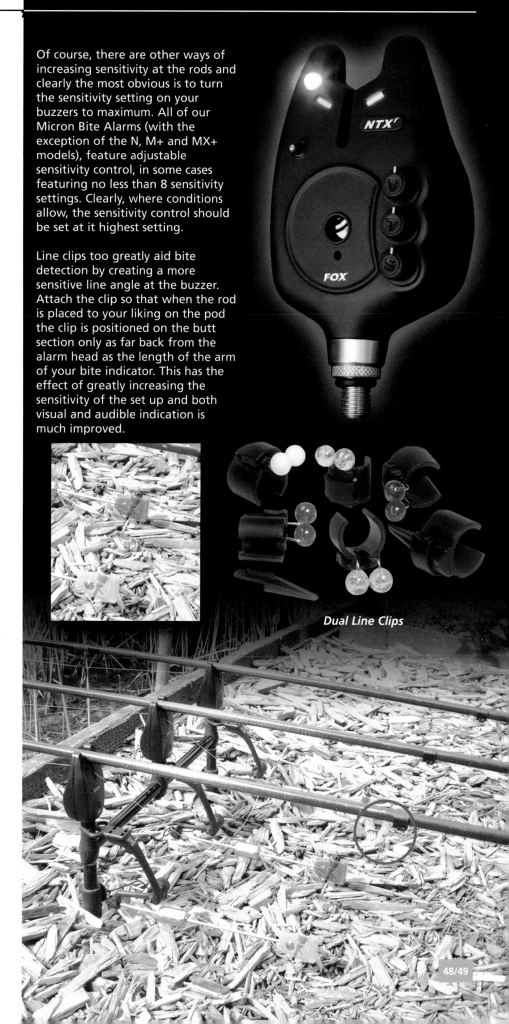

*Dual Line Clips*

## CHAPTER 3. BITE DETECTION

As well as increasing the sensitivity at the buzzer there are a number of different types of bite indicators designed to show drop back bites. They fall into two main categories: fixed arm indicators such as Swingers, and Hangers. Unfortunately, it is hard to argue either system is better than the other - in fact if you were to take a survey amongst anglers as to whether they preferred Swingers or Hangers the result would probably be 50/50. For 90% of angling situations the decision falls purely down to personal preference. However, it is probably fair to say there are certain angling situations when one can outscore the other.

Our range of Hangers are very popular and in certain angling situations are as sensitive, if not more so, than the Swinger. The design of the hanger range of products closely follows the original idea of the bobbin indicator that started life way back in the 60s and 70s so if you like it represents a more traditional style of bite detection.

So when should you use a hanger? Well for the most part Fox Swingers are as sensitive as you will ever need but in certain angling situations a Hanger may be more suitable. For instance:

Margin fishing calls for the most delicate presentation of them all. Carp that are creeping around the margins are at their most wary and the mere sight of the line under water will have them fleeing from the swim. Once again the ideal presentation is to have as much of your main line as possible lying on the bottom. However, when you are fishing right under the tips, even the slightest amount of weight on the line will tend to lift the main line off the bottom so we suggest that a Hanger with no add-on weights attached, or best of all, a SpringLok.

This is the lightest Hanger in the range and is ultra sensitive, making it perfect for fishing at close range or in the margins. When slack line fishing away from the margins it is best to use the lightest bite

indicator you can find, at the same time maintaining an excellent level of sensitivity. In such a situation a Butt Hanger or Illuminated Hanger carrying either one or two of the removable weights is ideal.

*Fox Core Lite Hanger*

A sliding collar weight allows the loading of the Swinger to be increased or decreased depending on the range fished at.

Some anglers argue that Swingers are the most versatile of all bite indicators as they allow a much greater degree of fine-tuning. By sliding the weight along the arm in the direction of the buzzer, sensitivity can be gradually increased. The closer it is to the buzzer the less down force is imposed on the line and the more sensitive the set up becomes. While this is true to a certain extent, for general all round fishing for distances up to 80 yards a Swinger or Hanger will suffice.

However, Swingers really come into their own when you start fishing at extreme range. True, it is to your advantage to disguise the line as we showed in the previous chapter but when you are casting over 100 metres then you need to be much more aware of what is going on at the business end of the gear out there on the lakebed. Bear in mind that when you

are fishing over 100 metres from the bank, the last twenty metres or so will generally be on the lakebed. By sliding the weight towards the light reactive indicator head on the Swinger, more tension will be imposed upon the main line and sensitivity will actually be improved. More importantly, by loading the weight close to the Swinger head we maximise the indication if we receive a drop back bite and these can be common at range.

Extreme range fishing, such as is commonly practiced abroad on the massive inland seas and reservoirs such as Raduta Lake in Romania or Lac du Der-Chantecoq and Foret d'Orient in France, may mean that you will be fishing at 200m plus. When you start taking baits out to extreme range using a boat then even greater sensitivity is required if you are not going

to miss a take. As well as using braided reel line such as Submerge Plus, we also suggest that you use Euro Swingers to increase sensitivity at these extreme ranges. Remember, the Euro Swinger and Illuminated Euro Swinger both feature not only a 56g sliding collar weight but further tension can be dialled into the set up thanks to the spring loaded tension facility. This allows you to increase the amount of force being applied to the line over the buzzers so that bites at ranges of 300-400m or more are instantly detected.

To summarise: for margin and slack line fishing use a Hanger; for extreme range use a Swinger. For all round fishing the choice is yours, but ensure you use the minimum amount of weight you can get away with which will also show a drop back bite.

## CHAPTER 3. BITE DETECTION

Naturally bite detection and the sensitivity of your set up will greatly depend on the efficiency of your rig so to round off this chapter let's just take a look at a couple of rigs whose effectiveness depends on a combi rig style of presentation using our new Rigidity hooklink material.

Rigidity comes in two different breaking strains,15lb and 25lb and is purpose designed for tying modern anti eject stiff rigs. Ultra stiff rigs are especially difficult for a taking carp to eject. The reason for this is that, unlike supple braids or nylons, stiff rigs do not fold back on themselves with the result that the hook stays inside the carp's mouth that much longer… and the longer it's in there, the more chance it has of getting a hold.

Fox Consultant, Ian 'Chilly' Chillcott is a staunch advocate of stiff rigs that incorporate ultra stiff boom sections. Here is one of Chilly's favourite combi rigs that uses 25lb Rigidity for this role.

To tie the rig you will need: some 25lb Rigidity; some soft yet supple braid, here we have used Snare; a size 7 Swivel and a 4.5mm Oval Rig Ring.

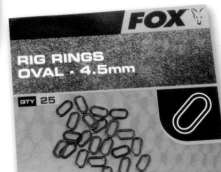

*"Chilly with a big common taken on a combi rig"*

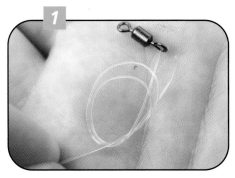

1. First we'll tie the boom section. Cut off a section of 25lb Rigidity and then thread one end through the ring in the size 7 swivel. Form a simple overhand knot to create a large loop.

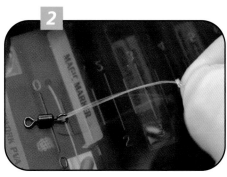

2. Cut off the tag end and blob the cut end with a lighter. The finished loop should be 2.5 to 3cm.

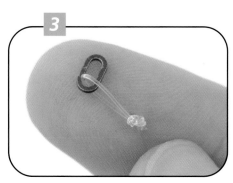

3. Tie the other end to the 4.5mm rig ring using another overhand loop. The loop formed should be small and compact, unlike the loop knot at the other end of the Rigidity

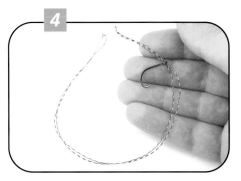

4. To form the hair take a section of ultra fine braid such as 25lb Snare and form a loop using an ordinary overhand knot. Thread it through the eye of the hook.

5. Now form a Knotless Knot to secure the hook and pull tight. The finished braided section that attaches the hook and forms the hair will look like this. Note: you can make up loads of these well in advance to produce an instant quick-change system.

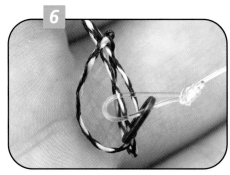

6. Now we need to attach the short braided section to the stiff boom section. Thread the loop of braid through the rig ring and carefully thread the boom section through the loop. Snug it down against the rig ring.

You will note that we have advised a very large loop knot at the swivel. I am not sure if he is being modest but this came about by accident (he says) when Chilly was in a rush to tie a rig after spotting feeding fish eating his bait. In his haste he tied a much larger loop than he'd intended but the result was that he had a fish on the bank. Testing the rig later he noticed that when fished with a snowman set up that sinks very slowly the slow sinking hookbait pushed the loop back through the swivel until it hit the knot. Chilly soon saw the advantage of this; not only was there vertical movement at the loop but also horizontal movement as the loop passed through the swivel in the first few milliseconds after a pick up, a time when the fish is feeling for resistance. The larger loop makes all this possible and it has a great deal to recommend it.

• Finally use a couple of Fox Tension Bars to test the knots and to straighten the Rigidity.

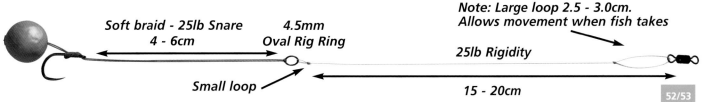

Soft braid - 25lb Snare
4 - 6cm

4.5mm
Oval Rig Ring

Small loop

Note: Large loop 2.5 - 3.0cm.
Allows movement when fish takes

25lb Rigidity

15 - 20cm

Here's another rig that uses 25lb Rigidity to form the boom section of another type of combi rig. Rigidity, has a tendency to curl up in large loops particularly when it is taken straight from the spool.

To straighten it steam the boom section under tension (use two Tension Bars and make sure not to get your fingers caught in the steam!) over a boiling kettle for a few seconds*. After removing from the steam, maintain tension while the boom section cools down.

Once straightened you will find that Rigidity creates a nice straight, ultra-stiff boom section that is ideal for all types of combi rig presentations. You can make up plenty in advance of your session and keep them stored in your rig wallet.

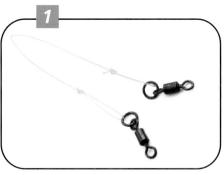

1. First form the boom section by looping the Rigidity to the rings in the two ringed swivels using standard overhand loop knots.

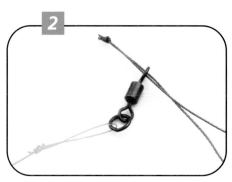

2. Now take a six inch length of 25lb braid and tie an overhand knot to join the two free ends together. Pass this through the swivel in the size 7 ringed swivel.

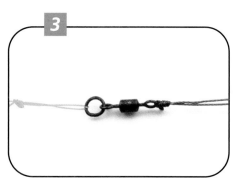

3. Using a three turn blood knot tie the knotted end to the swivel, cut away the tag ends.

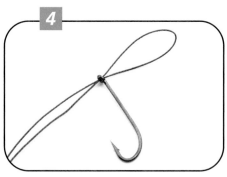

4. Pass the loop of braid up through the eye of the size 6 Fox Series 4 hook.

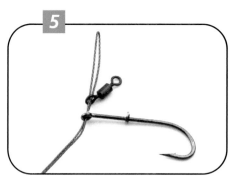

5. Now thread the mini rig swivel onto the loop of braid and locate the 2mm rig ring on the shank of the hook.

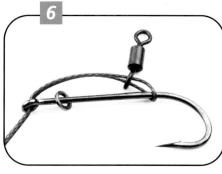

6. Taking care that neither the mini swivel or the rig ring fall off, pass the loop of braid over the point of the hook and position it opposite the point of the hook.

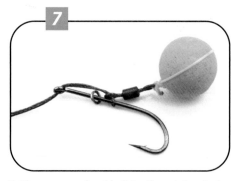

7. Tie a pop-up hookbait to the mini swivel. Should you need to replace a hook at any time simply slip the loop off the hook, take off the mini swivel and the rig ring and replace the hook before repeating steps 5-7.

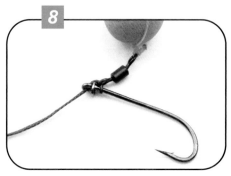

8. During the fight the braid loop will slide down the hook shank to rest against the eye of the hook. Don't worry about this as the small rig ring that you have positioned on the hook shank will protect the braid during the fight. The rig can be reset with a fresh hookbait prior to recasting.

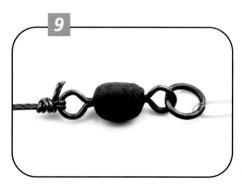

9. If you need a counter weight to overcome the buoyancy of the pop-up hookbait use Hi-SG Tungsten Putty moulded around the barrel of the ringed swivel.

The rest of the combi rig is a version of the Multi Rig, which was devised by Mike Kavanagh.

As well as the 25lb Rigidity used to form the boom section, you will also need: a section of 15lb braid, two size 7 ringed swivels, a mini rig swivel, a 2mm rig ring and a size 6 Arma-Point LS.

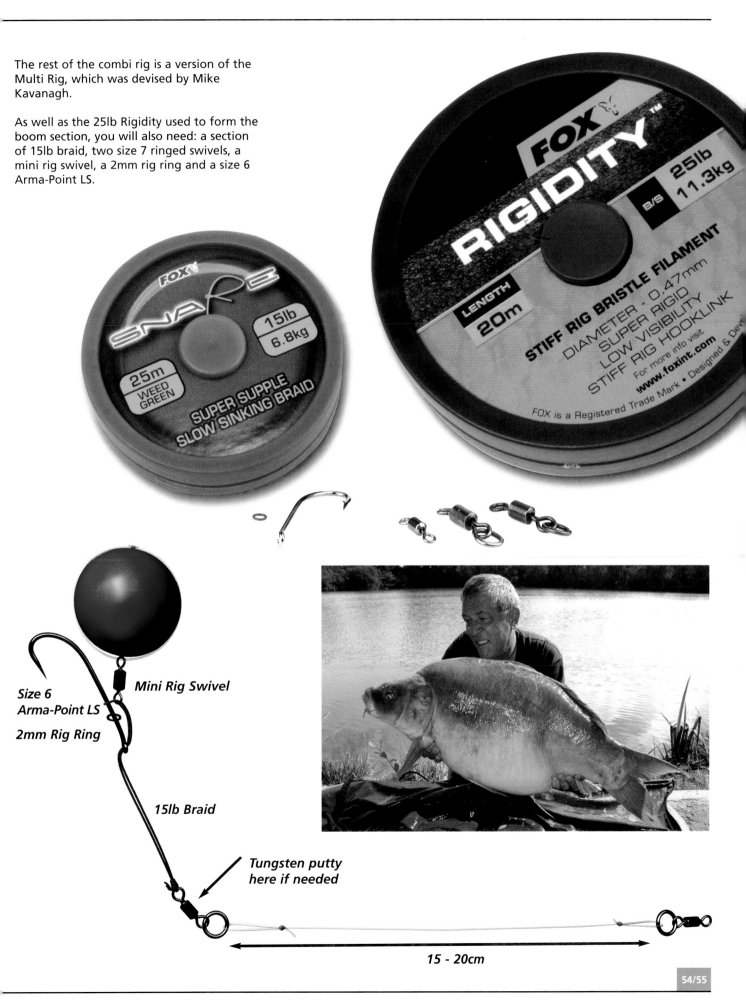

**Mini Rig Swivel**

**Size 6 Arma-Point LS**

**2mm Rig Ring**

**15lb Braid**

**Tungsten putty here if needed**

15 - 20cm

54/55

* This operation should not be attempted by children under the age of 16 unless supervised by an adult.

# CHAPTER 4

## Some Useful Knots + Crimping

*"Incorporating loops into stiff rigs creates freedom and flexibility"*

Modern carp rigs are all about flexibility and suppleness. Even ultra stiff hooklink materials like Rigidity are intended to be fished with a degree of flexibility built in. This can be acheived by incorporating a Flexi Ring Swivel into the rig, or by tying a loop at the swivel end. Some anglers go as far as to use both in their rigs.

The most common loop knot, often seen illustrated in magazines, is the standard single overhand loop knot. Unfortunately we have to say that with the exception of 25lb Rigidity we have our reservations about this knot, as it is in effect self-strangling. That is to say as the knot comes under pressure during a fight or in hit and hold situations the coils bed down harder and harder upon themselves to the point where they constrict each other and start to degrade the integrity of the material. A standard single overhand loop tied in all but a handful of materials weakens the hooklink considerably as the knot strangles itself to bursting point.

25lb Rigidity is affected to a degree by this knot, but we have found that thanks to the way the nylon is constructed the material is able to stand up to the pressures that are imposed when the knot begins to tighten. However, a sudden impact will still be enough to put the knot at risk. There are many better alternatives so please read on.

Many members of the Fox Team will have witnessed instances of the single overhand knot letting go under tension or when a sudden shock is applied. It is certainly no good when you are fishing in weed, as the fish only has to shake its head while buried in the weed bed for the nylon hooklink to part like cotton at the loop knot.

Image 1 shows the standard one turn overhand loop knot. This is the weakest of all the loop knots and is not to be recommended for most hooklink materials. That said, there are one or two ways you can increase knot strength if using the overhand knot. Firstly do not pull equally hard on both ends of the knot but instead semi tighten the knot then pull hard on the standing end (the hooklink itself rather than the free tag end) of the knot to tighten. This causes less of a strangulation effect and makes for a stronger knot.

Image 2 is a double overhand knot which is a considerable improvement over the standard one turn knot. As you can see, this time the swivel is passed through the loop twice. Though this is preferable to the one turn knot it still has the tendency to strangle itself and thus become weak. Again the advice about pulling the line tight applies.

Image 3 shows one of the best loop knots around. It is called the Figure of Eight Knot. The line is given less opportunity to bite down upon itself as the knot is tightened so there is less chance of the knot strangling itself. Follow the route of the red Magic Marker to see how the knot is formed.

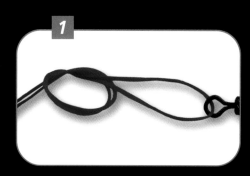
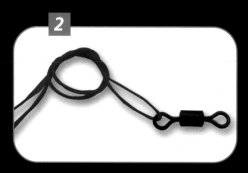
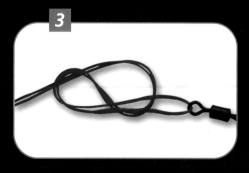

Now this knot, the Rapala Knot, is the business, without doubt the best loop knot there is. It will not strangle itself and it will certainly not give way under a sudden jerk, nor under a steady pull. It retains about 90% of the line's original strength and should be the knot of choice whenever you wish to tie a loop in nylon.

Although the Rapala Knot isn't the easiest knot to tie, once you have mastered it you won't have cause to worry about a loop knot ever again. If the waters you fish are weedy or you are likely to encounter snags or underwater obstructions the Rapala Knot really is the only option as it will never let you down.

There is of course an alternative in the form of a Flexi Ring swivel but we know that some anglers prefer the larger loop that a hand-tied knot can give. If you want to see an action sequence of this knot being formed take a look at the Fox Guide to Millennium Carping DVD's. This is how to tie the knot:

## Rapala Knot

**1**

*"Tie an overhand knot in the line then thread the tag end through the eye of the swivel".*

**2**

*"Pass the tag end back through the loop formed by the overhand knot".*

**3**

*"Pass the tag end around the line twice.... "*

**4**

*".. before passing it back through the loop that was formed by the over hand knot".*

**5**

*"Tuck the knot by taking the tag end back through the loop shown".*

**6**

*"Moisten the knot whilst pulling on the main line to form the loop".*

The members of the Fox Carp Team are given free reign to experiment with various items of tackle in the other ranges of Fox tackle. Though the range of carp gear is very extensive there are times when products crossover from one species to another and a typical example are the Fox Crimping Pliers, Sleeves and associated accessories.

For years Pike anglers have used crimps to secure hooks and other items to wire traces - as knotting wire can be problematic. Crimping offers a quick, convenient way of creating loops and securing swivels, hooks and other items without the need for knots. As crimps rely on compression to form the join, crimps are not really suited to braids or very fine monofilament.

The most obvious use for crimps is to form a loop in strong nylon, creating boom sections for stiff rigs. For this we suggest you use the 20lb crimps as the smaller bore makes them ideal for the diameters used. The sequence on the right shows how to go about this.

You can also use crimps to create rigs such as the Drop-Down Rig that we featured in the Fox Guide to Carp Rigs. Here's the Drop Down rig with the crimp securing the hook and forming a loop in which the bait, mounted on a ring, can sit.

**1**

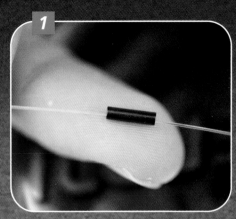

*"Thread the crimp on to the Fluorocarbon main line..."*

**2**

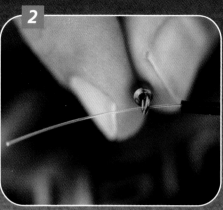

*"...before passing the line through the eye of the swivel".*

**3**

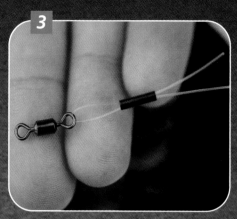

*"Then take the tag end of line back on itself and through the crimp as shown".*

**4**

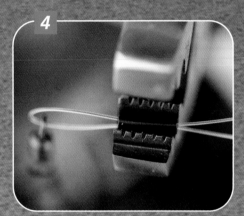

*"Place the crimp in the jaws of the crimping pliers".*

**5**

*"Apply compression to the crimp by squeezing the pliers then trim the tag end".*

**6**

*"The finished article looks like this. It is worth forming a blob in the tag end so it cannot slip under pressure".*

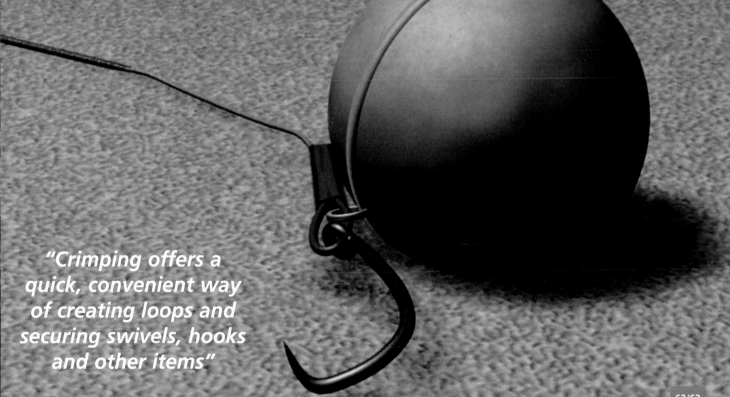

**"Crimping offers a quick, convenient way of creating loops and securing swivels, hooks and other items"**

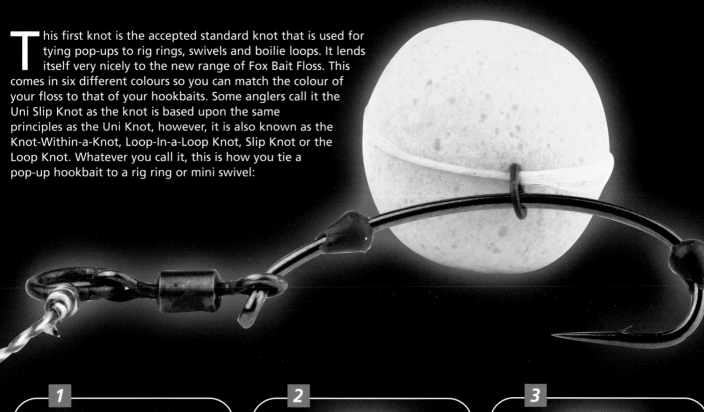

This first knot is the accepted standard knot that is used for tying pop-ups to rig rings, swivels and boilie loops. It lends itself very nicely to the new range of Fox Bait Floss. This comes in six different colours so you can match the colour of your floss to that of your hookbaits. Some anglers call it the Uni Slip Knot as the knot is based upon the same principles as the Uni Knot, however, it is also known as the Knot-Within-a-Knot, Loop-In-a-Loop Knot, Slip Knot or the Loop Knot. Whatever you call it, this is how you tie a pop-up hookbait to a rig ring or mini swivel:

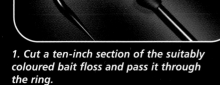

1. Cut a ten-inch section of the suitably coloured bait floss and pass it through the ring.

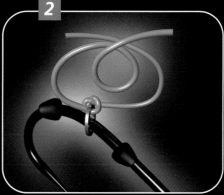

2. Pass the two ends over each other to form a large loop, and then repeat the process to form a smaller loop within the large loop.

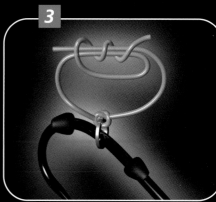

3. Pass one of the free ends twice or three time over the two loops, as if forming a Uni Knot.

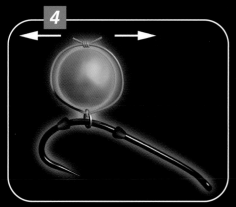

4. Place your hookbait on a suitable surface where it will not roll about all over the place, such as in a fold in your sleeping bag, and then position the loop around the hookbait.

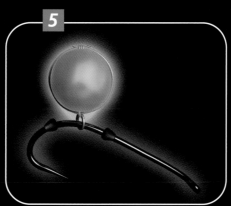

5. Gradually tighten the knot by pulling on the free ends. You will note that the loop starts to close around the boilie. Once it is in position to your liking, pull hard on the free ends to tighten the knot and hold the hook-bait securely in place

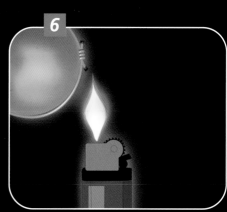

6. Trim off the excess and singe the two cut ends carefully with flame from a cigarette lighter.

* This operation should not be attempted by children under the age of 16 unless supervised by an adult.

Another method of attaching baits, especially pop-ups, is to use the lassoing method in conjunction with the knotless knot. This is a superb system for all types of bait and it can be used in all manner of angling situations. We like the quick-change aspect of the rig as one pop-up hookbait can be changed for another very quickly. You can even change the size of your hookbait, switching from, say, a 12mm pop-up to an 18mm version in a few seconds without having to cut off the old bait and tie on the new one. We recommend that it is used with coated hooklink materials or one of our Linx range of hooklink braids. The new coated hook link Coretex is ideal for this knot and in order to illustrate the knot we'll now look at a rig that uses the knot to great effect.

The rig we are about to tie is the BlowBack Rig. For the rig to work effectively it needs to be used in conjunction with a pop-up hookbait which we attach by lassoing.

This is a superb rig with the most amazing hooking properties thanks in no small part to the long shank Arma Point LS hook. This pattern of hook is often regarded as somewhat old fashioned and it is certainly the most under rated hook in the Fox range. However, many of our consultants regard the Arma Point LS as an unsung hero, one that has put fish on the bank when conditions are difficult when other patterns may have failed. Due to the dynamics of the way a long straight-shanked hook behaves in the mouth they are especially difficult to eject.

To tie the rig we recommend: a size 6 Arma Point LS; a small 2mm rig ring; a rubber rig stop and a section of of our awesome Coretx – the best coated hooklink available!

*"This is a superb rig with the most amazing hooking properties thanks in no small part to the long shank Arma Point LS hook"*

**FOX**

1. Cut off a 20-inch section of Coretex and strip away several inches of outer coat to reveal the 20lb breaking strain braid within.

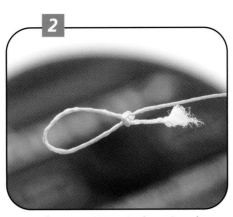

2. Now form a Uni Knot in the stripped section and trim the knot to make it nice and tidy. Pull the knot tightly to leave an adjustable loop at the end of the Coretex.

3. Now position your pop-up hookbait within the loop and carefully draw the loop closed around it.

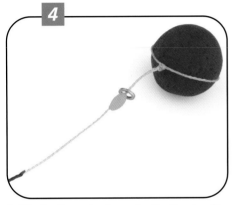

4. Slip the 2mm rig ring onto the Coretex (it should not be tied to the hooklink but free to move along it), followed by the rubber rig stop.

5. Thread the end of the Coretex through the eye of the size 6 series Arma Point LS hook.

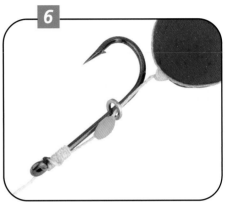

6. Pass the hook point through the 2mm rig ring and then holding the hookbait tightly in the correct position, form the knotless knot to secure the hook. Ensure that both the rig ring and the rig stop are on the bait side of the knot.

7. Finally slide the rubber rig stop up the shank to butt up against the 2mm rig ring, so that the ring is positioned roughly opposite the hook point.

8. Attach a size 7 Flexi Ring Swivel to the opposite end of the Coretex to finish off the rig.

9. When you need to change hookbaits simply pop the old one out of the loop, enlarge the size of the loop slightly to accommodate the new bait, then position the new pop-up in the loop and pull the loop tight again.

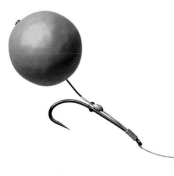

14cm

66/67

Here's a set up that comprises the rig, lead and the leadcore behind the lead.

This rig incorporates one of the most effective hookers in the business, the 360 Degree Rig which we looked at previously. It is also perfect for slack line fishing as it uses leadcore not only for the hooklink, but also behind the lead acting to pin down the tackle completely. Fished along the lines we mentioned in the section on slack line fishing this rig represents the ultimate in concealment and disguise. You may feel that it is a bit long winded to tie but don't forget, it encompasses the entire End Zone, not just the rig itself.

First we shall create a smooth, free running lead using the new Slik Ring Kit, which was actually designed to create a friction-free marker float set ups. However the kit is equally effective for creating a running lead set-up. The ring itself has a low friction ceramic centre made from polished Zirconium, which allows the line to whistle through with minimum resistance or friction that could cause suspicion in a taking carp, causing it to drop the bait before a run occurred. The kit also includes a couple of quick-change speed links for easy swapping of lead weight and a large diameter bead to absorb the shock of the cast. To create the free running set-up it's best to use a fairly heavy lead. In addition to the lead and Slik Ring Kit, you will also need a baiting needle and a tail rubber from the safety lead clip or some silicone tubing.

*1. Use a baiting needle to force a tail rubber from a lead safety clip over the swivel in the lead.*

*2. Next attach the Speed Link to the hole in the Slik Ring and attach it in turn to the top eye of the lead swivel.*

*3. Now carefully fold the soft tail rubber over the link and swivel to create a tangle-free running lead.*

*• With the new Fox Slik Run Rings resistance is minimised to such an extent that a taking carp should not be able to detect the weight so easily, even if you are using leadcore behind the lead.*

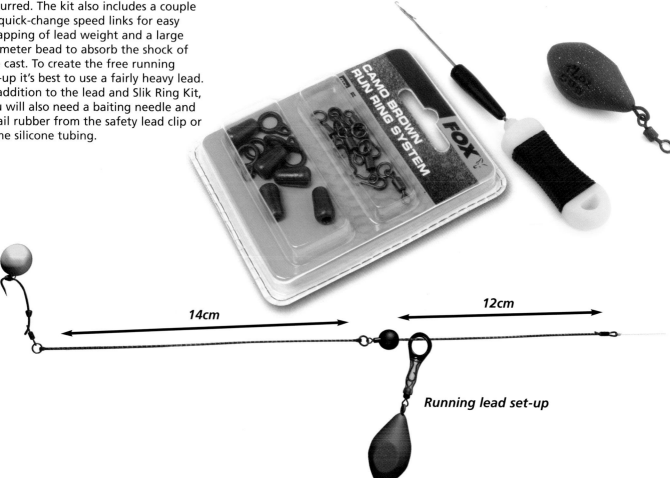

14cm

12cm

*Running lead set-up*

Now we need to form the business end of the rig itself. The process and items needed to create the rig are very similar to the 360 degree rig we looked at in Chapter 2 but there are some subtle variations.

To create the 'business' end of the rig you will need the following components:
Size 11 Flexi Ring Swivel; Arma Point LSC size 6 hook; Rubber Rig and Ring Stops; a bulk spool of 45lb Adaptive Camouflage Leadcore and a size 7 Flexi Ring Swivel.

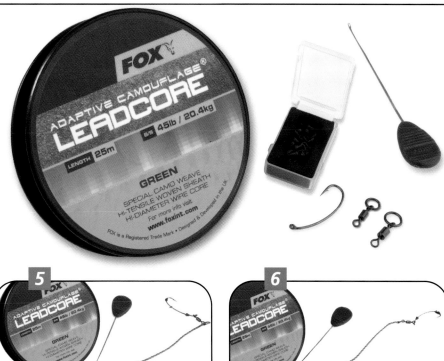

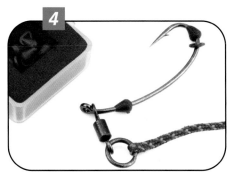

4. Take an 18-inch length of leadcore and splice to the ring of one of Flexi Ring swivels, before threading the swivel over the hook and forming the 360 Degree Rig.

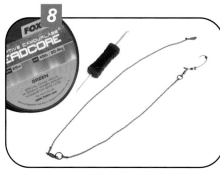

5. Splice the ringed end of the other Flexi ring swivel to the length of lead core.

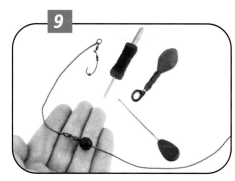

6. Take another length of lead core and splice it to the eye of the Flexi Ring swivel.

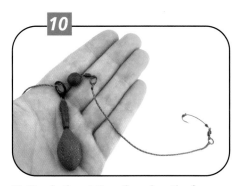

7. In the opposite end of the lead core splice a small, neat loop.

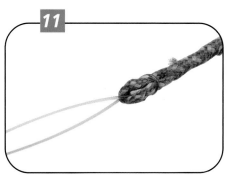

8. The rig is almost finished now and should be looking like this. The two lengths of lead core ensure the entire End Zone lies along the bottom.

9. Use a splicing needle to pull the leadcore through the central bore in the high diameter rubber bead from the Slik ring kit.

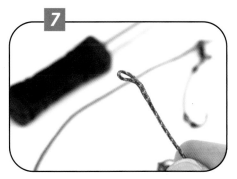

10. Nearly there! Now thread on the free running lead set up created earlier.

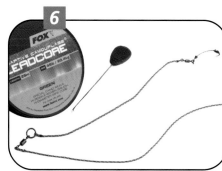

11. Now its simply a case of attaching the mainline to the loop in the leadcore with the loop to loop knot.

12. Finally, attach a small pop-up to the ring using the appropriate coloured bait floss and the rig is ready to go.

# *CHAPTER 5*

## *Modern Pop-Up Rigs*

At Fox we are constantly looking to add and improve upon our range of rig accessories as we freely accept that rigs and methods are constantly evolving. We are naturally aware that anglers need to keep their fingers on the pulse of what's happening and we hope that our range of accessories fills the gaps in most anglers tackle needs. Rig development is important and we will always strive to bring you the best and most innovative rig accessories going in order that you, the angler, can create ever more inventive and subtle rigs. However, before getting too carried away can we just utter a word of caution here? It's something we touched on in the first book but we feel the point needs reinforcing.

Anyone who has been carping for some time, as most of our Carp Team have, will tell you that rigs are just one small part of an overall picture and it is a mistake to regard them as the number one priority in our sport. Unfortunately many youngsters and newcomers to carp fishing seem to think that if they've got the latest super-rig then everything else is of secondary importance. They skip lightly over the subject of bait, location, watercraft and the host of other vital aspects of carp fishing that they need to master in order to be successful and concentrate solely on their rigs.

Most of the Fox Carp Team tend to rely on relatively simple rigs in which they have total confidence. OK, everyone has a favourite rig and there will inevitably be a measure of disagreement as to which is the best, but don't forget, you can only invent the wheel once and anything that follows thereafter is just a variation on a theme. You can be as complicated or as simple in your choice of rig as you like but at the end of the day it's just a hookbait that is attached in some way to the hook.

It is all too easy to blame the rig for the fact that you may not be getting takes but in fact it is far more likely to be down to other factors if you are blanking. It could be due to poor location or an inferior bait or any combination of several factors, yet many anglers make the mistake of blaming their rig first, refusing to acknowledge in other areas of their fishing.

Carp fishing is not as hard as some people would have you believe, especially where rigs are concerned. If you are in the right spot, using a bait that the carp want to eat, the rig doesn't need to be too complicated. The harder a fish feeds the easier it is to catch. Take that to its logical conclusion and you will realise that success starts with a good bait, not a good rig. Match a great rig to a poor quality bait and you may have the odd fish but your action will soon tail off once the fish stop eating your bait. Substitute the poor bait for a superb one and long-term success is assured.

Most rigs evolve through a linear thought process. The angler sees a problem in his mind's eye and resolves to find a rig that will beat the problem. Let's assume that the first time it is cast out the rig catches. Does that make it the solution to the problem? Probably not. One swallow doesn't make a summer just as one take doesn't make a rig. Too often anglers accept what they think might be happening as fact, without confirming what is actually happening. Writers, and to a lesser extent the tackle trade would like you to believe that rigs are all a matter of black and white. The fact is, it's all shades of grey.

Carp anglers are obsessed with rigs and they are always looking for the 'Ultimate Rig'. Sadly, like the ultimate bait, it doesn't exist! When the hair rig was first invented by Lenny Middleton it changed the face of carp angling forever. Buzzers sprang to life and reels came alive all over the country. From a take comprising a few twitches we were now getting full blooded, heart-stopping runs. It was awesome! At the time everybody regarded Lenny's baby as the 'ultimate' rig. Yet with hindsight we now know that it could be (and has been) improved upon.

Nowadays we have all kinds of weird and wonderful rigs and since the original hair was conceived literally hundreds of permutations of the hair rig have been invented. It has to be said that many have proved to be pale imitations of the original. Nevertheless, the frantic search for the 'ultimate rig' continues. We won't claim that any of the rigs in this book are the 'ultimate' but they should all put you in with a great chance of landing plenty of fish, provided you always keep in mind that rigs aren't the be-all and end-all of carp fishing.

The MKII Swimmer rig we are about to look at isn't a full on pop-up rig, although a pop-up bait is used. As you can see from the diagram below, the eye of the hook is anchored to the bottom and the bait sits directly above this about 15mm off the bottom. The rig offers the superior hooking associated with a pop-up rig and also keeps the hook point free from weed, silt or other debris that could obstruct it. Where the rig can score is on hard fished waters where fish have become wary of pop-ups.

The rig works on the same principle as the 360 Degree Rig in that regardless of the angle that the carp approaches from, when the fish mouths the bait the hook spins and lodges lightly in the middle of the bottom lip.

To tie this rig you are going to need the following items from the Fox carp fishing range of tackle. We suggest a long shanked hook for this rig, either a size 6 Arma Point LS or LSC. You will also need a size 7 Flexi Ring Swivel, a size 11 Flexi Rig Swivel, and a length of 25lb Coretex coated hooklink braid.

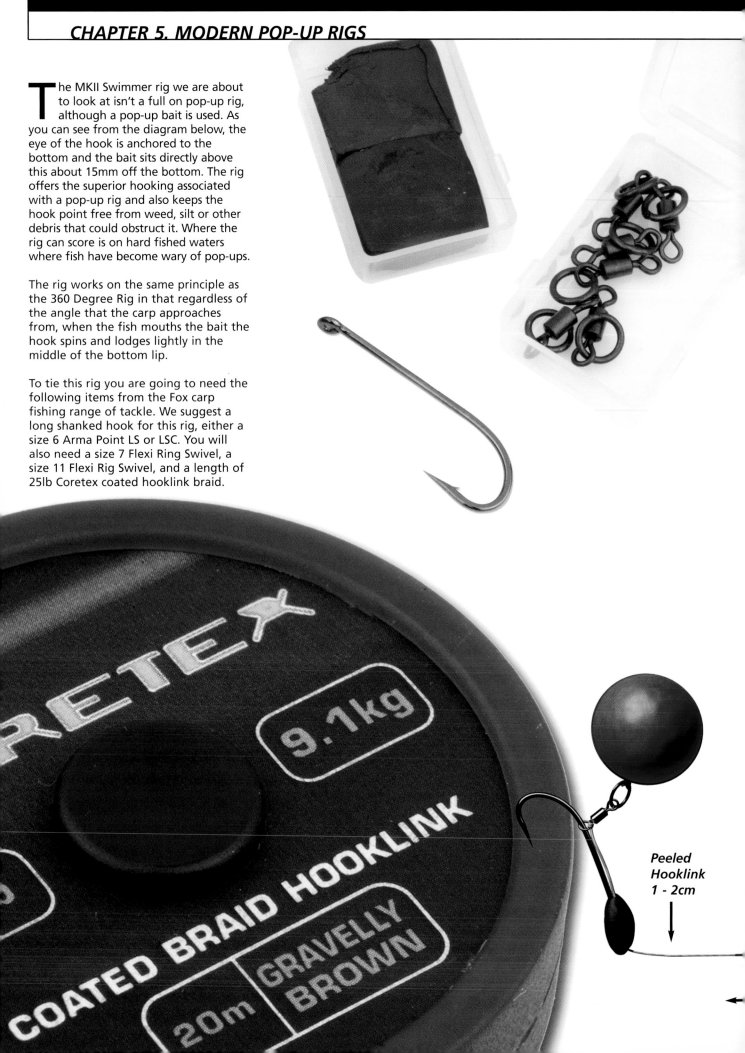

Peeled
Hooklink
1 - 2cm

1. Strip off the outer coating of the Coretex to reveal a section of inner braid.

2. Using a simple 3-turn tucked blood knot, tie the braid to the swivel on the size 11 Flexi Ring Swivel. NOTE: do not tie it to the eye of the swivel but attach it around the root of the eye where it enters the barrel.

3. Next slip the hook point through the eye of the swivel.

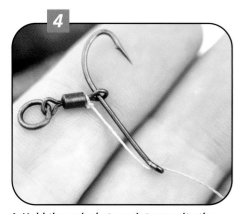

4. Hold the swivel at a point opposite the point of the hook.

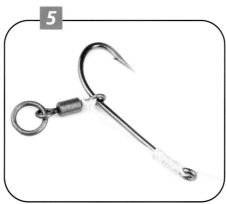

5. Form a knotless knot to secure the swivel. You should have about 2cm of uncoated braid showing below the eye of the hook. If not peel back a few more millimetres until the required length of braid is revealed.

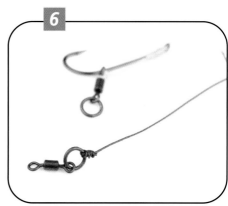

6. Attach the other end of the hooklink to the ring in a size 7 Flexi ring Swivel.

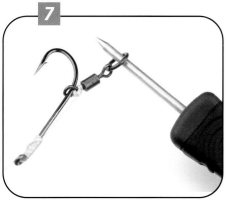

7. Use Tension Bars through the ring of the ringed swivels to tighten the knots and test the hooklink.

8. Now using the loop-in-a-loop knot we illustrated in the last chapter, attach your pop-up hookbait to the ring of the size 11 swivel sitting on the hook shank.

9. Finally mould Hi-SG Tungsten Putty around the eye of the hook and the whipping formed by the knotless knot. This should ensure that the rig sits tight to the bottom in an almost upright positionon the lakebed.

*25lb Coretex Coated Hooklink*

*13cm*

Although this chapter is primarily about pop-ups rigs, this next rig can also be adapted for bottom baits or snowman set ups. In fact, it is arguably the most versatile rig ever devised as you can change hooks, hairs and hair arrangements at the drop of a hat, without having to break down or re-tie the rig itself. For instance, you can change from a pop-up set up, incorporating a tied-on bait, to a long-hair bottom bait rig in a matter of seconds while still keeping the hooklink the same. It is the brainchild of long-time carper, Essex rig expert Mike Kavanagh, the man who gave us the original Stiff Rig. The Multi-Rig is another product of Mike's highly inventive brain.

Incidentally, you may think that this and some of the other rigs in this book are too time consuming, however, an extra couple of minutes spent on presentation may spell the difference between success and failure. Sure some rigs are a bit complicated and fiddly to tie but the extra time and effort will be worth it.

In the photo shown below you can see the basic concept for yourself. It shows two versions of the rig, tied using our new Coretex coated braid. One rig is baited with a double bottom bait set up on a braided hair. The rig to the left features a tied-on pop-up hookbait tied to a 3mm rig ring.

Over the page we will show you how to tie both versions of the rig. However, before we start making the rig we will make the hair and bait which is mounted on the hook. As making the hairs can be time consuming, it is good idea if lots are prepared at home in advance (perhaps of differing lengths in case you wish to use multiple hookbaits) and taken with you. To make the hair you will need a spool of leadcore and splicing needle plus a 3mm rig ring.

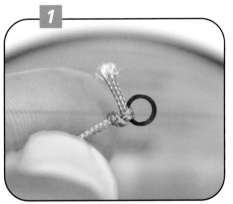

1. First tie a braided hair for bottom bait presentations. Cut a length of leadcore outer braid and tie it to a 3mm Teflon-coated Rig Ring using a 2-turn blood knot.

2. Trim off the tag end and singe the end with a flame to make it nice and tidy.

3. Now pass a splicing needle through for about 1.5cm. The further away you introduce the needle from the rig ring the longer the hair will be.

4. Splice a small loop, big enough to hold a hair stop.

5. Mount the bait/baits onto the hair and add a Boilie Prop.

## The Multi-Rig

To tie the rig you will need some Coretex coated braid, a couple of stainless steel rig rings, one 3mm and one 1.5mm, a Flexi Swivel Ring, some leadcore outer braid (the leadcore has been removed throughout), and the hook of your choice. The rig can be tied with virtually any hook pattern, the only limiting factor being that it must have an eye large enough to allow doubled coated braid to pass through.

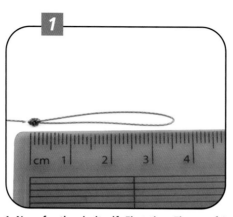

*1. Now for the rig itself. First tie a Figure of 8 Loop Knot in the end of your Coretex hooklink material. Depending on the size of the hook you are using, the length of the loop should be between 3-4cm.*

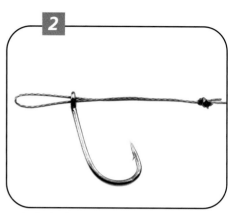

*2. Pinch the loop tight between forefinger and thumb and pass the loop of braid up through the eye of the hook.*

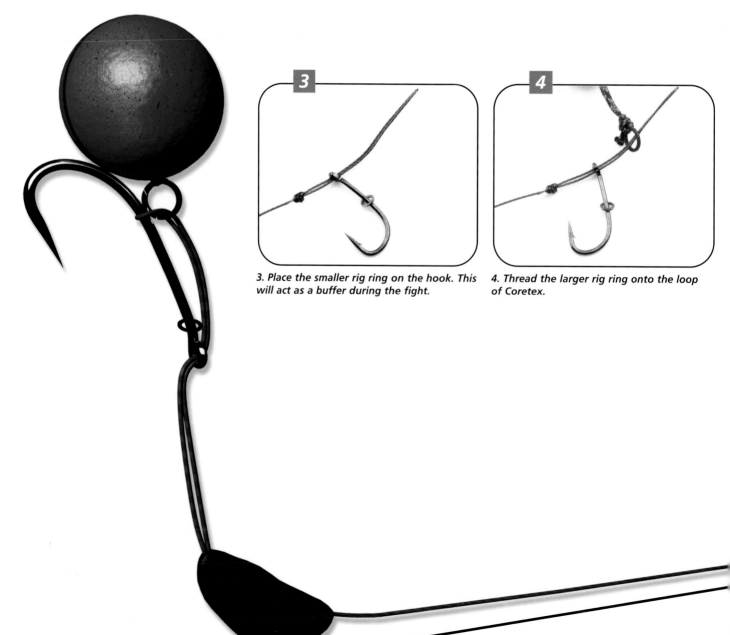

*3. Place the smaller rig ring on the hook. This will act as a buffer during the fight.*

*4. Thread the larger rig ring onto the loop of Coretex.*

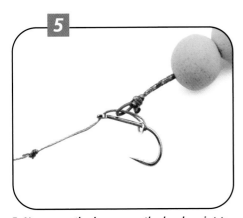

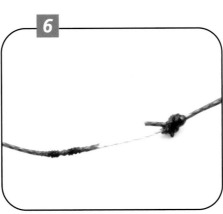

5. Now pass the loop over the hook point to form a D section along the lines of a standard D-Rig. Adjust the size of the D section according to how you wish to present your bait(s). Generally speaking it is best to have the end of the loop opposite the point of the hook. In this photo we show the rig using double bottom baits on a braided hair.

6. For a stiff set up leave the coating intact throughout the hooklink; for a more supple, Combi Rig type of set up, peel away a small section of coating below the loop knot to form a hinge.

7. To tie the rig as a pop-up presentation tie your pop-up hookbait to the rig ring on the Coretex using the loop-in-a-loop knot.

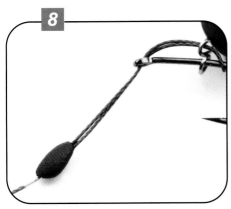

8. Mould Hi-SG Tungsten Putty around the loop knot to counter the buoyancy of the hookbait.

9. Finally attach a Flexi Swivel Ring to the opposite end of the hooklink.

10. During the fight the pressure on the hooklink will pull the loop tight against the eye of the hook. As you can see here, the small rig ring now acts as a buffer, preventing damage to the hooklink whilst it is under pressure. The loop can be easily returned to its former position after unhooking the fish.

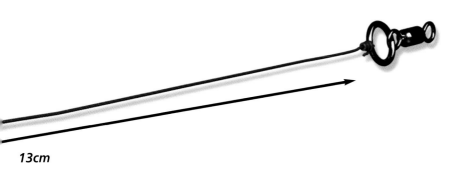

13cm

The full Withy Pool Rig would appear to be the most useless fish hooker of all time. For a start it fails the much vaunted palm test every time! Well let us reassure you that this rig really does the business and it is arguably one of the best pop-up rigs ever invented.

*"The Withy Pool Rig is the brainchild of Steve Renyard"*

The Withy Pool Rig is the brainchild of Steve Renyard, once a regular angler on the famous Bedfordshire water after which he named the rig. Steve was one of the most successful anglers ever to fish the lake, thanks in no small part to his brainchild.

As with many of the rigs in this series, there are several variations in methods of tying the rig so what follows is just one way of tying it. You will note that in the pictures we have used a short shanked, wide gape hook. Other anglers prefer longer shanked hooks. In practice we have found that both the Arma Point SSP and SSBP work well with this rig.

Please note: This rig will not work with anything other than a buoyant pop-up hookbait.

The mechanics of the rig dictate that the hook and hookbait must turn and hold, something it clearly it cannot do it if is lying on the lakebed attached to a standard bottom bait.

To tie the rig you will need the following:
• A size 6 Fox SSBP hook
• A size 7 Flexi Ring Swivel
• A rubber rig 'n' ring stop
• Some Hi-SG Tungsten Putty
• A section of 1.2-0.4 Fox Shrink Tube
• A coated hooklink such as 25lb Coretex.
• A cork!

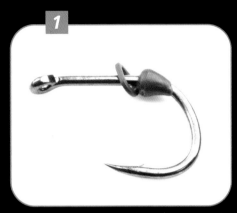

1. Before you go any further position the rig ring and the rubber buffer stop on the shank of the hook.

2. Tie the Coretex directly to the eye of the hook using a twice-through-the-eye 3-turn Grinner Knot.

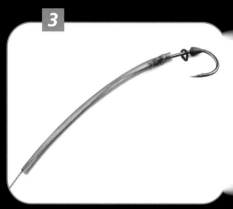

3. Now take a length of 1.2-0.4mm of shrink tubing. Thread it onto the hooklink and then position it over the eye of the hook*.

4. Now to shrink the tube correctly. Wrap the tube around a wine bottle cork and shrink it down over the steam from a boiling kettle. Take care not to scald your fingers!*

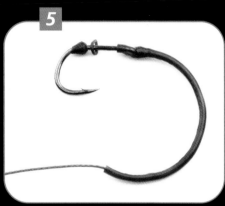

5. After the shrink tube has reduced in size as much as possible plunge it into cold water to maintain its curved shape.

6. Tie on your hookbait using the loop-in-a-loop knot.

* This operation should not be attempted by children under the age of 16 unless supervised by an adult.

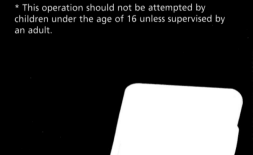

9. We now need to position a counter weight. Some anglers use a tungsten shot immediately below the end of the shrink tube. Alternatively you can use one of our Kwik Change Pop-Up Weights. However, we like to use Hi-SG Tungsten Putty, which we mould around the bottom of the shrink tube under the hookbait.

8. Attach the opposite end of the hooklink to the ring in the Flexi Ring Swivel.

There are loads of variations of the original Withy Pool Rig that have sprung up over the years including the Half Withy. Tying the Half Withy is simple, follow the same steps as we showed you on the previous page but instead of using the whole section of shrink tube, cut it in half. Again, shrink the shrink tube around the cork to produce the characteristic curve in the tube. This creates a similar rig but has a slightly more acute angle.

On many waters where long shanked hooks are banned, using a length of shrink tubing can create a safe alternative to what have been commonly known as bent hooks.

The angle of the shrink tube can be altered from the 180 degree presentation in the original Withy Pool rig to the Right-Angled Withy as used by Mike Winstone of Horseshoe Lake fame. Altering the angle of the presentation to a shallower more acute angle creates a rig that is difficult for the fish to eject, whereas the original Withy Pool rig with its 180 degree bend is more likely to prick the fish as it backs off the bait.

FOX

## Right Angled Withy

To form the Right Angled Withy simply shrink the tube at a right angle over the steam. With both these variations you need to add counter weight just below the end of the shrink tube. Depending on how you think the fish are picking up the hookbait, choose either a heavy counter weight so that the rig is fished over-shotted or go for a lighter weight with critical-balancing in mind.

We'll show you a step-by-step sequence of the Right Angled Withy as it illustrates nicely a slight variation that can be applied to all these rigs.

For this rig we are going to use a size 6 Arma-Point SSP hook and a braid hooklink and will use the knotless knot to form the hair. Straight away you will be able to see the differences between this and the Withy Pool Rig.

12cm

1. First of all tie a loop for the boilie stop in the end of the braid. We recommend 20lb Snare for this rig. Now use the knotless knot to attach the hook.

2. Next take section of 1.2-0.4mm shrink tube and cut it in half.

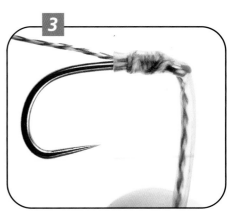

3. Slide it onto the Snare then position it over the eye of the hook and the whipping on the shank. Shrink it into place, forming a right angle as shown.

4. Attach your hookbait by piercing it with a boilie needle and threading it onto the loop. Secure in place with a boilie stop. You can match the colour of your stop to that of your bait thanks to our coloured boilie stops.

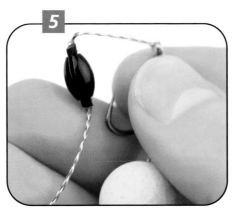

5. Now position a Kwik Change Pop-Up Weight at the end of the shrink tube.

6. Tie the other end of the Snare to a size 7 Flexi Ring Swivel

82/83

## CHAPTER 5. MODERN POP-UP RIGS

Pop-up presentations appear to rule the roost in carp fishing these days and with good reason, as they can be blisteringly effective. The nature of a pop-up means the hook sits above the bottom clear of any weed or other debris that could obstruct the hook point. A pop-up fished correctly on a good rig, ensures the hook is suspended in the prime hooking position. This is why fish caught on pop-up rigs are hooked in the middle of the bottom lip and why generally speaking, hook holds on pop-ups tend to be better than those obtained with bottom bait presentations. The important thing to remember is that the pop-up must sit correctly so you must always test your rig in the margins or a tub of water before you cast it out.

It is always worth remembering a pop-up needn't be fished an inch or two inches off bottom. Recently a lot of anglers have been presenting pop-ups mid water on a kind of short zig rig. In fact, in 2005 Brian Jarrett and Dave Gawthorn won the British Carp Championships by fishing single hook baits two feet off bottom above a large bed of bait they had spodded in six feet of water. Although fishing hook baits this high in the water requires different rigs it does go to show that we shouldn't feel restricted by the height at which our pop-ups are presented.

It would be hard for anyone to argue that a pop-up is a 'natural' presentation and on some waters they can blow very quickly, but here Ian Chillcott gives you his thoughts on why pop-ups can be so effective:

*"Although pop-ups cannot ever be described as a 'natural' presentation they are devastatingly effective. It has been well publicised that I have used Stiff rigs to great effect over the last years, sometimes with the hook bait popped-up 2-3 inches off bottom. The improved hook holds and the difficulty fish have in ejecting a good pop-up rig means they play a big part in my angling.*

*I cannot be sure why the fish do not associate what a human would think is an extremely obvious way of distinguishing a hook bait, but I do have ideas and theories. If you think about it, a popped-up bait only appears so if it is viewed from ground level. If you look over the top at the bait there is no real way of knowing how far off the bottom the bait is. Contrary to popular belief carp do not swim round tight to the lake bed. Most of the time the fish will sit at a level in the water that they feel most comfortable at – more often than not dictated by temperature – which isn't normally tight to the lake bed. Therefore a feeding carp will tend to approach the hook bait from slightly above the bait rather than along the bottom, even if it is popped up a couple of inches".*

There is no getting away from the fact that pop-ups work and they are highly recommended but, as with all things in carp fishing, the fish can become suspicious and they can have a built in scare factor on some hard fished day ticket waters where the fish are bombarded with pop-ups day after day.

Don't automatically reach for the tub of pop-ups the minute you are ready to bait up. It's almost a habit with a lot of anglers, but while it is undeniable that there are times when a pop-up will out fish other presentations, at the same time there will be days when semi buoyant or standard bottom baits are more effective.

The successful carp angler is constantly thinking about his presentation and will be ready to adapt and at times even drastically change it in order to overcome any presentation problems he might be facing. As we have often pointed out, rig choice is often a matter of horses for courses and a rig that works like a dream on one water can fail abysmally on another so keep an open mind.

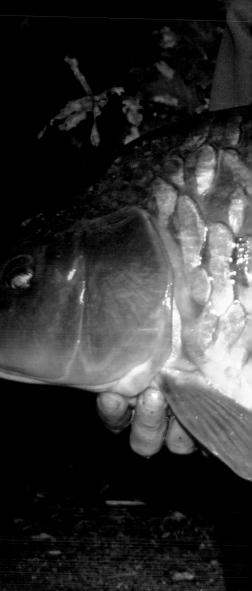

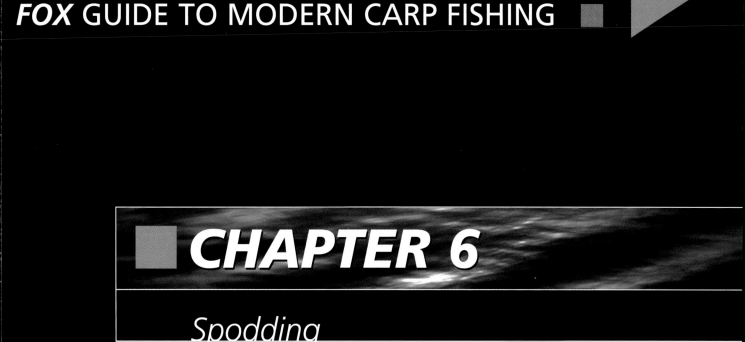

# CHAPTER 6

*Spodding*

Spodding has undergone something of a revolution in the last few years, and it is probably fair to say that the majority of carp anglers now go equipped to spod large or small quantities of bait when they go for a session. The knock on effect on the weights of carp, up and down the country has been astonishing with massive growth rates recorded on many different fisheries.

Prior to spodding the most common methods of introducing bait was via a Catapult or Throwing Stick; both have serious disadvantages. Catapults are a quick and efficient way to introduce feed but with the exception of boilies, propelling any bait in excess of 50 metres is nigh on impossible. Throwing sticks can also deliver boilies to ranges over 100 metres but cannot be used effectively with any other bait.

No doubt many of you reading this will have experienced the annoyance of seagulls picking up boilies in mid air or as soon as they hit the surface. On many carp lakes gulls have come to recognize the swooshing sound of a throwing stick in action and they quickly gather in a massive flock, ready to pick up the baits in flight. Those baits that escape mid-air interception are followed down to the surface where they are picked off as soon as they hit the surface.

On well stocked venues, laying down large quantities of bait can lead to big multiple catches. On this type of water, the very act of spodding can act as a dinner gong and carp will often come to the sound of the spod hitting the waters surface, even nudging it and taking the bait on the drop as it empties! However, it is fair to say that spods do have their time and place - casting one near big carp on low stocked venues will invariably see the carp making a rapid departure from the area!

Spodding is unquestionably a very effective tactic, which in the right hands and on the right venue can produce huge hauls of fish. In fact, with the exception of bait boats, there is arguably no quicker method of introducing a large amount of bait in such a short amount of time.

This baiting revolution has led to the development of various specialised, dedicated tackle items devoted to the practice; everything from the spods themselves through to purpose built rods, reels and lines. All of these items have been designed to make spodding easier and over the next few pages we will look at how best to go about spodding; it takes a lot of dedication, and a great deal of determination to build up a bed of bait by firing out a spod a hundred yards or more, time and time again. However, it is ultimately highly satisfying and can be a very successful approach indeed.

## CHAPTER 6. SPODDING

Although Spods come in a variety of shapes and sizes, it is probably fair to say any spod fully laden with bait is going to be substantially heavier than the leads you are likely to be casting. Therefore, it is a good idea to buy an inexpensive, purpose built spod rod that is designed to handle the strain. You don't need to spend a fortune to acquire a good spod rod. Fox's Warrior Spod Rod, retails for less than £65 so it's not going to break the bank. In addition it is designed to do just one specific job, cast heavy spods.

The Warrior has a test curve of 5.5lb, yet under casting pressure the twelve foot rod assumes a nice easy and progressive action. It will take loads of abuse and can withstand the strain of casting 6oz spods almost indefinitely.

You will find life a lot easier if you use a big pit reels for spodding work. They make casting and retrieving so much easier and quicker and for the most part they are built to take the stresses and strains imposed by continuous casting with heavy loads.

You will find that using braided mainline on the reel you use for spodding makes the task somewhat easier. The newly released Exocet Spod Braid is perfect for the job. This is a braided mainline specifically developed for heavy duty spod work. Incorporating ultra strong bonded Dyneema filaments with a breaking strain of over 30lbs, Exocet Spod Braid is incredibly tough and hard wearing and for most applications can be used without a shock leader. The tight weave and low diameter allow smooth, extreme range casting with minimal wind knots and tangles.

The buoyant fluorescent yellow filaments ensure the braid is highly visible in all conditions – this can prove invaluable when casting baited rods to the spod as it empties, preventing tangles and line crossovers.

You will certainly be able to cast a heavy spod a lot further with braid, as it possesses none of the elasticity associated with nylon. Braid transmits the power of the cast more directly and the build up of power is improved. In consequence the spod goes further!

One word of warning about using braid, which we have stressed before. Make sure you protect your casting finger (usually the index finger of the hand holding the reel end of the rod). Braid can cut your finger badly and if you are in for a bout of prolonged spodding you will soon make the finger tip very sore if you do not take steps to protect it. It is a good idea to buy a leather fingerstall from the chemists, or alternatively try a neoprene or soft leather golf glove.

In addition, if you are using braided mainline always ensure that the clutch is fully tightened to the max before casting out. If there is any give, the line will inevitably slip as the power of the cast is piled on. As it slips across your fingertip, it will cut the flesh to the bone.
Be warned!

You can use a spod for all modern day-to-day fishing situations but it is especially recommended for laying down a carpet of bait on a feature that is marked with a marker float. Similarly you can use it to cast to visible features such as an island, the far bank treeline or holes in the in the weed. It's a good idea to use the line clip on your reel to ensure that you don't continually overcast the spot or to ensure the spod doesn't end up in the trees on the far bank. To prevent damaging the line in the line clip put a section of power gum or pole elastic inside the line clip. Alternatively fold a piece of thin card over the line prior to putting it in the clip.

Bear in mind that if you are using braid as your main line, the clip may stop the cast too abruptly and can actually jerk the spod back towards you due to the lack of stretch in the braid.
To prevent this remember to watch the spod while it is in the air, follow the line of flight with the rod tip after the cast is made. Once the spod is in flight lift the rod to a more upright position once the cast is made. When you feel the line hit the reel clip, push the rod forward and downward to a horizontal position, following through on the cast.
This softens the jerky impact of the braid in the clip and does not pull the cast backwards towards you.

## CHAPTER 6. SPODDING

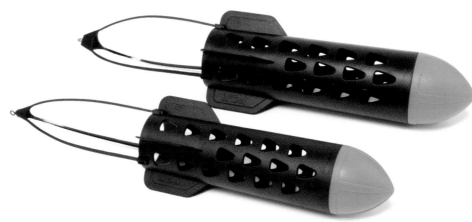

Here at Fox we have recently launched the awesome new range of Exocet spods. They are widely regarded by the industry experts as the best spods ever launched and will undoubtedly give you a very big edge in your spodding. By using cutting-edge Computer Aided Design the Exocet has been developed to fly as far and straight as possible. It has a tapered body for distance and accuracy and stiff harness that enables it to skip across the water's surface on the retrieve. The spod is available in Small and Large and there is also a new Boilie Rocket available from September 2010.

The Exocet comes supplied with three buoyant nose cones, which enables the spod to come to the surface very quickly after impact. This ensures the bait empties very quickly and also aid a much easier retrieve. Touches such as these make the task of spoddng a whole lot easier and will enable you to get a big bed of bait into the lake in no time at all.

1. The spod doesn't go deep on entry....

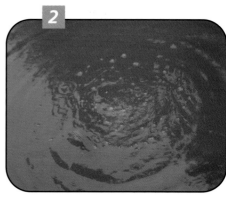

2. .. and starts rising to the surface quickly.

3. In under a second the spod has risen to the surface.

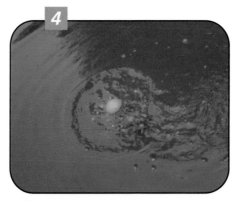

4. The spod starts to invert....

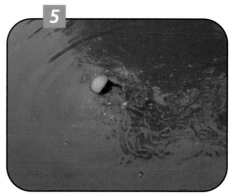

5. .. and the bait begins to release into the swim.

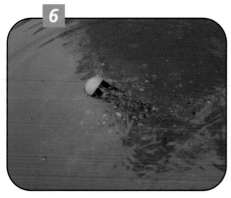

6. A slick of hemp oil forms around the spod.

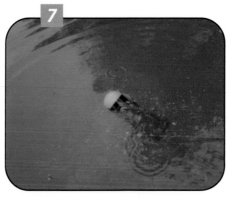

7. Twitching the spod speeds up the discharge process.

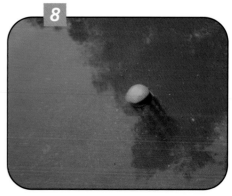

8. Just over three seconds and the spod is empty.

The Large Exocet weighs in excess of 6oz when loaded and is perfect for baiting up with large quantities of spod mix in a short period of time. Due to the heaviness of this spod, remember to always use a purpose-built spod rod to avoid any accidents from occurring.

The Small Exocet obviously doesn't hold as much bait as the Large model, and is design for extreme range baiting. Distances in excess of 170yds have been achieved with the Small Exocet and you really do need to see it to believe just how far and straight this little beauty will fly.

This small spod is perfect for introducing smaller bait quantities when fishing shorter sessions, for winter carping, long range spodding or simply for keeping the swim 'topped up'. It makes far less disturbance on impact and with a loaded casting weight of only around 3ozs it can be cast on a standard carp rod without requiring a shock leader unless long distances are being cast.

The size, number and shape of the teardrop vents are critical and these have been incorporated specifically to provide rapid bait discharge on impact with the water and ease of retrieve when winding in. This makes the introduction of big baited areas fast and efficient.

Both spods come supplied with parallel bore inserts that can be added should you wish to bait up with small items such as micro pellet and maggot or with a sloppy mix when fishing Zig Rigs. This eliminates the need to place tape around the spod like you would have to with other company's spods. This removes the need to place tape over body and allows the user to add water to increase casting weight, or to spod very wet 'soup' style mixes without undue bait loss.

The inserts also allow the spod to be filled with water and cast to the required mark before clipping up. This prevents bait from being spread around the swim while distance and accuracy is achieved.

When used without inserts the spod is fantastically easy to retrieve due to the enlarged vents which allow superb water exchange. During retrieval this provides an even pressure on the line resulting in perfect line lay. Many spods 'skip' along the surface which can put loose coils of line on the reel causing tangles and crack-offs on the cast.

## CHAPTER 6. SPODDING

Here are a few general points to consider when deciding whether or not to use a spod.

1. There are times when a spod definitely scares fish. The noise of the spod landing will have the effect not of attracting carp to the swim but physically driving them out of it and avoiding the area like the plague for some time afterwards.

2. Conversely on other lakes the noise of a spod does actually draw the carp's attention to the baited area and the bait going in around the marker float. Treat each water individually and if you aren't sure what the carp's reaction is likely to be to the noise of a spod crashing in repeatedly, err on the side of caution until you know different.

3. It is very easy to introduce too much bait in one spot, or too much bait overall. It should be remembered that a fully laden Fox Large Exocet Spod will hold six or seven ounces of bait such as hemp seed or groats. That's a lot of bait and you only need to cast out a dozen times and suddenly you find you've put in over five pounds of bait. That may not necessarily be a bad thing, but it is all too easy to get carried away.

4. A well designed spod allows you to put bait out further than almost any other type of propulsion system. If you really want to get baits of all kinds out a long, long way you will have to turn to a spod of some kind.

5. Always remember, once you've introduced bait into a swim you cannot take it out. When baiting with a spod introduce enough feed to get the fish interested but don't overfeed them. If things go well you can always top it up but you can never take it out.

6. Incidentally, here's another worthwhile tip though it's nothing to do with spodding. When you re-bait, especially if you are on a long session, always throw your old baits in the lake, into the same spot. It might be under a nearby tree or just a few yards out into open water, but make sure that three or four washed out baits go into that spot day after day. Then a couple of nights before you pull off, fish a single hook bait on that spot. Again you'll be astonished at how many carp you may pick up from an unlikely place.

7. Remember to pick out a prominent casting feature behind your marker float so that you can cast in the same direction after dark. With the line in the clip still, the spod will not land far out of position as long as you aim for the same casting mark each time.

"Leading UK team Fox member Steve Spurgeon with a cracking 45lb+ French mirror"

# CHAPTER 7

*Non Pop-Up Presentations*

In this chapter we are going to look at some of the best rigs for fishing with either a standard bottom bait or one that retains a degree of buoyancy yet is intended to be fished on the bottom rather than popped-up. However, before we go into detail it's important to first consider one or two other aspects of hookbait presentation.

To start with let's consider a piece of carp law that is widely accepted, namely that you should match the size of the bait to the size of the hook. OK, we don't have an argument with that but as is the case with all aspects of carp fishing, exceptions often prove the rule!

No doubt most of you tend to be guided by the accepted wisdom: using large hooks for big baits such as 20mm boilies and small hooks for smaller baits such as mini boilies or a single grain of maze or a tiger nut. Indeed, many of you probably think that a size 2 hook attached to a 14mm boilie looks a bit silly and a size 8, in theory, would seem to be much more effective. However, on some waters, where the carp are behaving in a particularly suspicious manner, going against the accepted practice can be very effective.

There are definitely occasions when the tactic of using a big hook with a small bait actually produces more fish. For instance, when using bolt rigs incorporating a heavy lead, a short hooklink and a small hookbait as illustrated here.

The small bait/big hook bolt rig tactic works on the principle of the fish picking up the hookbait then pricking itself against the heavy lead in conjunction with the short hooklink as it turns away. Such a rig is nothing new; it follows the bolt rig principle that is almost as old as carp fishing itself!

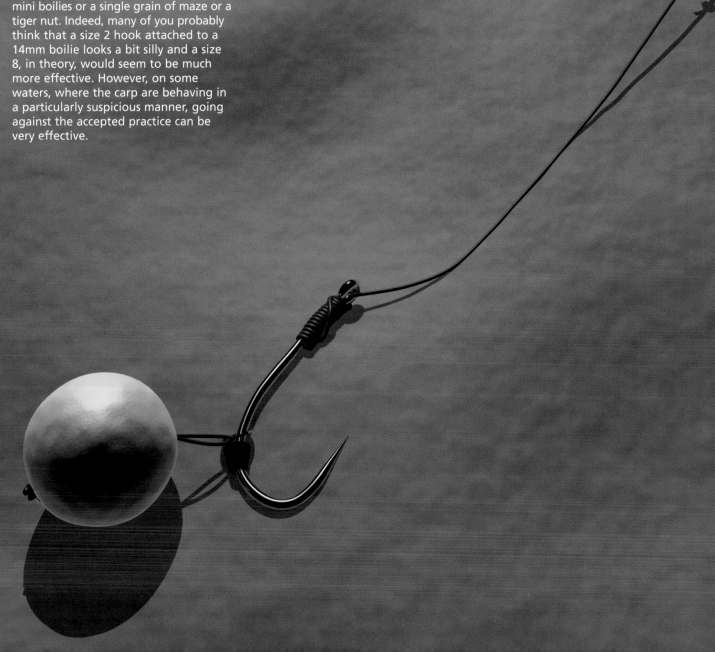

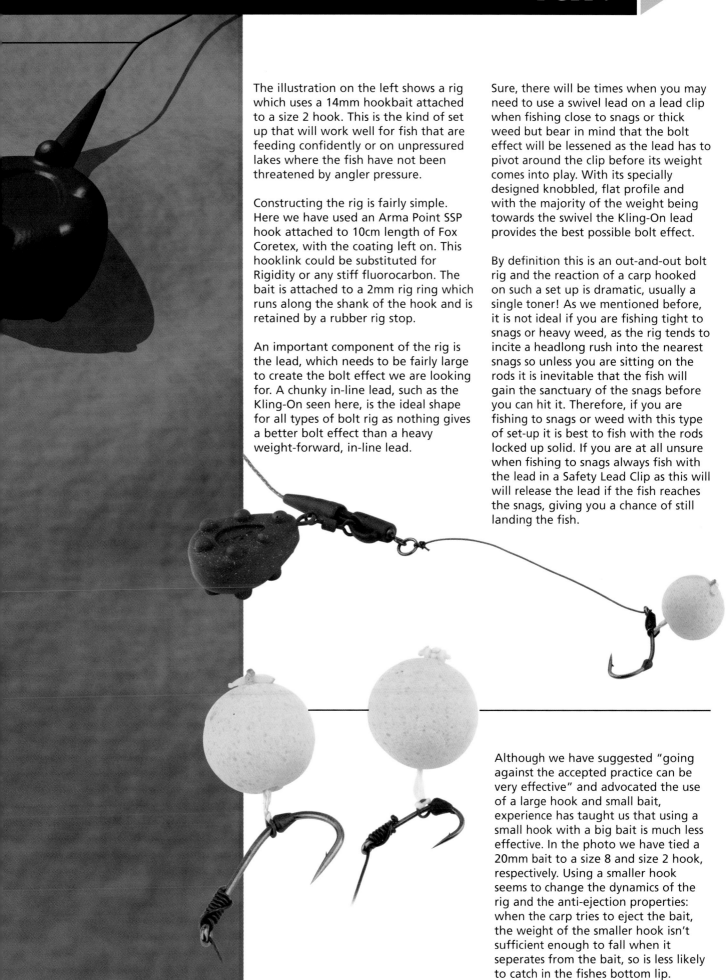

The illustration on the left shows a rig which uses a 14mm hookbait attached to a size 2 hook. This is the kind of set up that will work well for fish that are feeding confidently or on unpressured lakes where the fish have not been threatened by angler pressure.

Constructing the rig is fairly simple. Here we have used an Arma Point SSP hook attached to 10cm length of Fox Coretex, with the coating left on. This hooklink could be substituted for Rigidity or any stiff fluorocarbon. The bait is attached to a 2mm rig ring which runs along the shank of the hook and is retained by a rubber rig stop.

An important component of the rig is the lead, which needs to be fairly large to create the bolt effect we are looking for. A chunky in-line lead, such as the Kling-On seen here, is the ideal shape for all types of bolt rig as nothing gives a better bolt effect than a heavy weight-forward, in-line lead.

Sure, there will be times when you may need to use a swivel lead on a lead clip when fishing close to snags or thick weed but bear in mind that the bolt effect will be lessened as the lead has to pivot around the clip before its weight comes into play. With its specially designed knobbled, flat profile and with the majority of the weight being towards the swivel the Kling-On lead provides the best possible bolt effect.

By definition this is an out-and-out bolt rig and the reaction of a carp hooked on such a set up is dramatic, usually a single toner! As we mentioned before, it is not ideal if you are fishing tight to snags or heavy weed, as the rig tends to incite a headlong rush into the nearest snags so unless you are sitting on the rods it is inevitable that the fish will gain the sanctuary of the snags before you can hit it. Therefore, if you are fishing to snags or weed with this type of set-up it is best to fish with the rods locked up solid. If you are at all unsure when fishing to snags always fish with the lead in a Safety Lead Clip as this will will release the lead if the fish reaches the snags, giving you a chance of still landing the fish.

Although we have suggested "going against the accepted practice can be very effective" and advocated the use of a large hook and small bait, experience has taught us that using a small hook with a big bait is much less effective. In the photo we have tied a 20mm bait to a size 8 and size 2 hook, respectively. Using a smaller hook seems to change the dynamics of the rig and the anti-ejection properties: when the carp tries to eject the bait, the weight of the smaller hook isn't sufficient enough to fall when it seperates from the bait, so is less likely to catch in the fishes bottom lip.

## CHAPTER 7 NON POP-UP PRESENTATIONS

Let's move on now to look at a couple of presentations that use pop-ups to impart a degree of buoyancy yet are fished very close to the bottom. They are not really what you could call pop-up rigs but are more semi buoyant set ups that carp find very hard to deal with.

The first is a neat little rig that was first mooted by Keith Moors, a very inventive carp angler who was responsible for some of the most innovative rig ideas to come out of the 90s. I don't think the rig was given a name by Keith so for want of a better description we'll call it the Keith Moors Rig (how original!). It is a rig that has been around for quite a while yet it doesn't seem to get thecoverage it deserves. In effect it is basically a pop-up D-Rig but fished hard on the bottom.

In practice the rig will sit tight to the lakebed with the eye of the hook virtually resting on the bottom. However, the pop-up hookbait will ensure that the hook sits up off the bottom at a very aggressive angle. In addition the rig is very flexible thanks to the way it can pivot around the counterweight on the free end of the knot and you will find that it turns and holds instantly when the hookbait is taken into the mouth, or even when it is just mouthed by a cautious carp.

To tie this particular rig you will need a long shanked hook (straight or curved shank) such as an Arma Point LS or LSC. Most hooklink material will suffice, here we have used 25lb Snare although you could use Fluorocarbon such as 18lb Illusion. In addition you will need a size 7 Flexi Ring Swivel, a 2mm rig ring, some bait floss and a small kwik change pop up weight to counter the buoyancy of the hookbait.

*16cm of 25lb Snare or 18lb Illusion*

1. First tie a 3 turn grinner knot in the hooklink material leaving one end longer than the other.

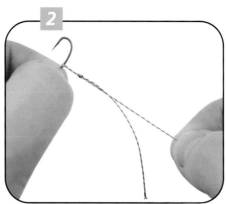

2. Place the loop formed by the grinner knot on the hook shank opposite the barb and pull the knot tightly closed. You can add a dab of super glue for extra security if you like.

3. Place the rig ring on both sections of hooklink material.

4. Pass both sections of hooklink down through the eye of the hook.

5. Using the longer section of hooklink, form a knotless Knot around the hook shank.

6. Add a Kwik Change Pop-Up weight to the shorter remaining section of the hooklink.

7. Trim the tag end on which the Kwik Change Pop Up weight is sitting.

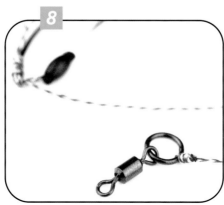

8. Attach the opposite end of the Snare to the ring in the Flexi Ring swivel.

9. Attach your bait to the ring with some bait floss and the rig is complete.

The next rig we are going to look at again uses a pop-up hook bait to give a certain amount of buoyancy to the set up. We showed you how to tie the standard Snowman Rig in the first book and as any of you who have read that will know, a standard snowman set up involves using a standard bottom bait and a buoyant pop-up bait on the same hair. The Snowman rig we set-up here is a slightly different version to the one we showed you in the first book. This version has been doing the business for some time now but it has been kept under wraps until quite recently and these photos show what we feel is the most effective way of tying the rig that we have yet discovered.

To tie the rig you will need the following: A Size 6 or 8 Fox Arma-Point LS hook, 25lb Fox Coretex or Insider coated braid, a sliver of 0.5mm silicon tube and a size 7 Flexi Ring Swivel.

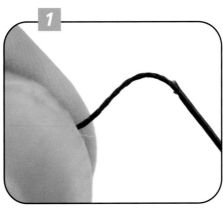

*1. First strip about 12cm of the outer plastic coating from the Coretex. You can do this very easily using your fingernails.*

*2. Mount the smaller pop-up bait on the baiting needle followed by the larger bottom bait.*

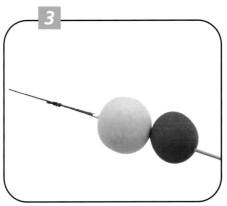

*3. Now tie a loop in the end of the stripped braid and attach your hookbaits using a lip-close baiting needle.*

*4. Now thread them onto the hair loop before securing them in place with a boilie stop.*

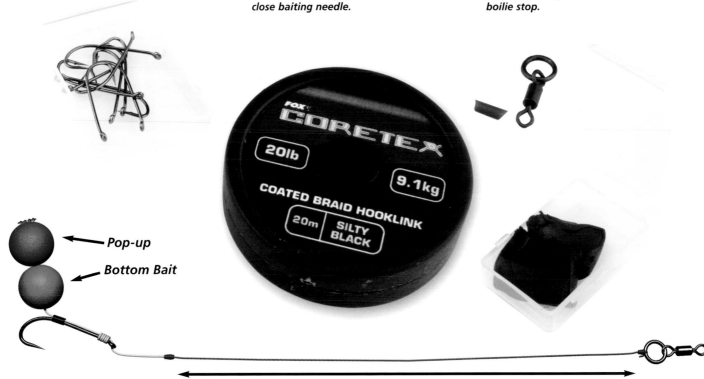

**Pop-up**

**Bottom Bait**

**20cm**

## Reverse Snowman Rig

The standard Snowman rig is one Fox Consultant Andy Little has used for years. However, on some of the waters Andy fished he found himself targeting carp that were able to eject the semi-buoyant presentations. Andy devised the Reverse Snowman rig where the pop up is mounted below the bottom bait. The advantage is the more buoyant of the two baits, which is now situated at the base of the hair, wants to enter the mouth first which makes the rig far harder for the fish to eject.

The reverse presentation is such a weird one that many anglers are scared of it but it can really work miracles on most waters. The dynamics of the rig are totally different to the standard snowman set up and in the carp's mouth the rig also behaves very differently. We strongly urge you to give this one a try as we think you'll be pleasantly surprised! If you're not convinced enough to give it a full blooded trial in actual fishing conditions, at least give it a test at home and you'll soon see what we mean when we tell you that it is radically different!

Tie the rig as you would the normal Snowman, always choosing a smaller pop-up and larger bottom bait that allows the rig to sink without the need for any additional weight. Mount the bottom bait first followed by the pop-up. When placing the pop-up on the hair do not go through the middle of the bait but approximately 1/3 to one side as shown below.

*This means the baits form a 'V' shape with the pop-up just supporting the weight of the standard bottom bait with the hook sitting just under the baits.*

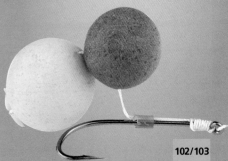

**5**

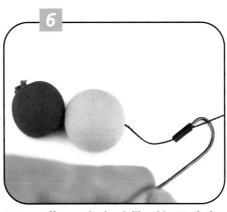

*5. Add a small section of silicone tubing to the hooklink.*

**6**

*6. Now offer up the hook like this. Work the hook through the silicone and onto the shank of the hook.*

**7**

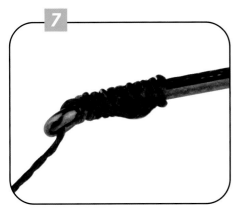

*7. Now thread the coated end of the braid down through the eye of the hook and form the knotless knot. The standard bottom bait should just be touching the bend of the hook.*

**8**

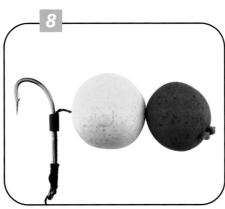

*8. Position the section of silicone opposite the point of the hook this changes the pivot point of the hair.*

**9**

*10. Next tie the end of the coated braid to the ring in the size 7 Flexi Ring Swivel. The overall length of the rig from the flexi ring swivel to eye of the hook should be about 20-25cm. Test the rig in the margins to ensure that it sinks slowly to the lakebed.*

**10**

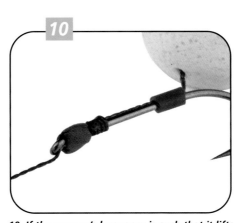

*10. If the pop-up's buoyancy is such that it lifts the bottom bait clear of the lakebed then bit by bit smear Hi-SG Tungsten Putty around the whipping of the knotless knot until the rig sinks ever so slowly. You will be surprised at how little Hi-SG you will need in order to counter the buoyancy of the pop-up.*

It seems as if a lot of anglers cannot see past pop-ups and they use them all the time, regardless of whether they are suitable for that particular water or not. In fact, many of the youngsters we meet on the bank simply don't want to know about bottom baits and they seem to regard them as old fashioned and ineffective. Nothing could be further from the truth and old hands like Andy Little, Chilly, Steve Spurgeon, Ken Townley and Chris Rose all totally accept that pop-ups are only one solution to a myriad of problems and they will happily use a bottom bait or a semi-buoyant bait when conditions dictate. They would never dream of using only pop-up rigs regardless of the conditions, the lakebed or the nature of the lake itself.

Choice of rig is very much a case of horses for courses as we have already pointed out, but many anglers make the mistake of thinking there is only one worthwhile type of presentation. Sure, all of us will readily use a pop-up if we think it is justified but there are equally as many angling situations when such a rig simply isn't necessary.

In fact, there may be times when it can have the opposite effect and work against you. Remember that carp quickly discover what's safe and what is not. If everyone on your lake is using pop-ups then it is inevitable that sooner or later the fish are going to start to become wary of any bait that is suspended just above the lakebed.

There is nothing whatsoever natural about a bait waving about some distance off the bottom. Originally pop-ups were used to combat bottom weed or silt, but some anglers were using pop-ups simply as an alternative presentation when fish were becoming suspicious of bottom baits.

The old saying of what goes around comes around applies here. It's a fact of carp fishing life that what works for you will eventually start to work against you and so it is with all types of rig presentation. The permutations seem almost endless so it is as well to keep in mind that some types of presentation may have a limited catching life until such time as they come back into favour again.

However, it is not always the carp that drive fads and fancies: often carp anglers change their presentation for no other reason that they fancy a change! That's not very logical, is it?

For the rest of this chapter we are going to rely on standard bottom baits. The effectiveness of all these rigs is dependent on a bottom bait/baits. Please note that these two rigs can only be used with a standard bottom bait. Any kind of built-in buoyancy will unbalance the rig completely and it will not be anything like as effective.

As you may recall, the original stiff rig was first suggested well over twenty years ago. The material of choice at the time was Amnesia 20lb, a fairly stiff nylon line intended for use as a shooting head backing line for fly-fishing. For the Stiff rig to be successful it needs a loop tied at the hooklink swivel. This allows the whole hooklink greater freedom of movement, producing a very flexible presentation that could be used to imitate the action of braided hooklinks but without the drawbacks of braids.

The stiff rig became a firm favourite with many anglers in those early days but experience showed that on some waters the carp wised up to it fairly quickly. A few of the thinkers in the carp world began searching for alternative presentations that retained the stiffness of the hooklink but with additional flexibility and suppleness at both the swivel and the hook end of the link itself. Thus the Drop-Down Rig was born in an attempt to ensure total and instant separation of hook from hookbait when the carp tried to spit out the rig.

The most critical few milliseconds of a take occur when the carp suddenly feels that all is not right with the food it has just taken into its mouth. It could be the hook or the feel of the hooklink on its lips but the change from a carp that is confidently feeding to one that thinks, get me out of here, takes just fractions of a second. What happens next determines whether you get a run or not.

1. The fish approaches the bait and sucks the hookbait up. Both the hook and bait enter the fishes mouth together.

2. When the fish feels that all is not right and trys to eject the bait two things can happen. The bait and hook do not seperate and both get ejected from the fishes mouth. For a rig to be effective the opposite must happen; upon ejection the hook and bait must seperate. As the force of the ejection acting on the hookbait comes into effect the hook point becomes lodged in the lower lip

3. When the hook first lodges in the lower lip it does not rely on the weight of the lead to achieve a hold; the mass of the hookbait attempting to exit the mouth is enough to cause the initial hook hold. It is only when the fish tries to move away - often at speed that the weight of your lead completes the sequence, lodging the hook further into the lip.

The next two rigs we are going to feature, the Drop-Down Rig and the Rotary Hook Rig are two modern carp set-ups that take full advantage of the separation of hook and bait and they are ideal when used on lakes that feature a hard gravel lakebed with little silt, weed or mud. The two rigs really work best when the bottom is clean with nothing to hinder the correct entry and exit of the hook and hookbait.

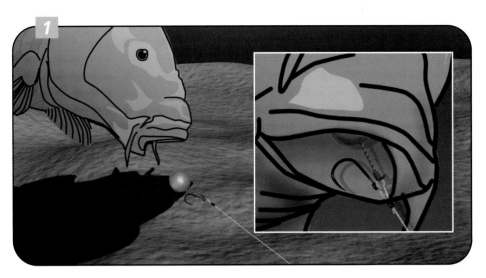

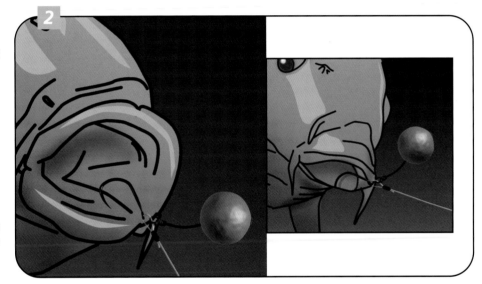

We were perfectly happy with the original Drop-Down Rig that we showed you in the first book but we have discovered one or two little tweaks that we think you will find beneficial. We therefore apologise for going over ground already covered but hope that you will be able to use the new developments to your advantage.

## "The inherent stiffness of Rigidity makes the rig extremely difficult for carp to eject"

The first point to note is that the new version of the rig uses the new Fox Rigidity in 25lb breaking strain. The inherent stiffness of the Rigidity makes the rig extremely difficult for carp to eject, as the hooklink material will not fold back on itself on ejection like many other types of hooklink.

As for the hook, well in our opinion when you are fishing with a 'floating' hook as is the case with the Drop-Down Rig, the shorter shank and the in-turned eye of the Series 2XS pattern is more effective as it gives a better initial pricking effect.

You will note that the hair set-up has been changed from a soft rubber bait band to a much stiffer braided hair. This improves the action of the rig because it forces the hook downwards and forwards on ejection thanks to the more rigid structure of the hair material.

Finally a quick word about the change in our recommended lead design. The shock effect of in-line leads is more instant and pronounced than that imparted by the same design lead fished swivel style in a safety clip. With this particular rig, which is intended to prick the fish lightly the instant the hook drops down onto the lower part of the mouth, the quicker you can achieve that initial bolt effect the better. That's why we have changed to an in-line lead.

These simple changes (i.e. Rigidity instead of Insider, a stiff braided hair, a change of hook pattern and a weight-forward in-line lead) represent something of an improvement over the original rig suggested to you in the first book.

We aren't saying that the previous version is not effective as it will work well on most waters, however, on the pressure waters where fish are just mouthing the bait suspiciously they will find that the ultra-stiff Rigidity in conjunction with the stiffer hair will be much harder to eject.

To tie the rig you will need the following: a length of the new 25lb Fox Rigidity, a size 4 Fox Series 2XS hook, a pre-tied braided hair tied to a 2mm rig ring with an overall length of 2-3cm (please refer to the section on the Multi Rig for details of how to tie braided hairs using the outer braid from our leadcore), a size 7 Flexi Ring Swivel, two 20lb Fox Crimps and a pair of crimping pliers.

1. First thread a 20lb crimp onto the end of a length of 25lb Rigidity.

2. Now thread the Rigidity up through the eye of the hook followed by the rig ring holding the braided hair.

4. Now pass the free end through the 20lb crimp to form a small loop.

4. Using the crimping pliers gently squeeze the crimp closed. You do not need to use excessive force, as it will hold with only gentle pressure. Note that neither the hook or hair are actually tied to the hooklink but are trapped within the loop.

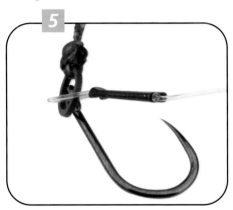

5. Trim off most of the tag end and singe with a flame.

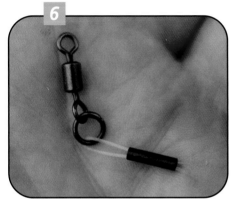

6. Slide the other 20lb crimp onto the Rigidity, pass it through the ring of the ringed swivel, and then back through the crimp again.

7. Cut and singe the tag end and crimp in place.

8. Position the hookbait or hookbaits (as shown here) on the braided hair, then locate a boilie stop in the loop at the end of the hair to hold the hookbait in place.

For the best results, we suggest using the Drop Down rig in conjunction with a heavy in-line weight-forward lead such as a 121g (4.25oz) Kling-On or Flat Pear. Incorporate a 1m length of Camo Leadcore behind the lead to keep everything pinned down in the End Zone. Alternatively use the same length of Loaded Tungsten Tubing.

Another curious rig that has accounted for some huge fish over the past couple of years is the Rotary Hook Rig. This is one of Andy Little's favourite rigs and he uses it not only when he is carp fishing but also when he targets barbel and chub. In actual fact the original rig evolved on the very hard lakes in the Black Country some twenty years ago or more but even though it has been around for all that time it has been kept very quiet by the specimen world, as it has been responsible for the downfall of some very large tench, barbel, chub and bream as well as accounting for numerous big carp.

The rig behaves in much the same way as does the Drop-Down rig in that hook and bait are totally independent of each other, not being attached to each other in any way and thus able to separate immediately and with devastating effect. Unlike the Drop-Down rig, we have found that most types of hooklink material are suitable for this set up. Stiff nylon, supple braids, semi-stiff coated braids or even standard nylon hooklinks such as 15lb or 12lb Soft Steel are all ideal and work well.

As the Rotary Hook Rig relies on the instant and effective separation of the hookbait from the hook at the moment of ejection it is ideal for ultra cautious fish that may suck in and blow out other rigs out without the hook getting a hold.

Tying the rig is simplicity itself but it is one of the most effective rigs you will ever encounter. To tie the rig you will need the following items. Hooklink of your choice (here we use 25lb Snare), a 2mm rig ring, some hair braid or bait floss (8lb Mega Silk is ideal for making supple hairs), two Float Braid Stops from the Fox Predator range, a size 5 Fox Arma-Point SR hook and a size 7 Flexi-Ring Swivel.

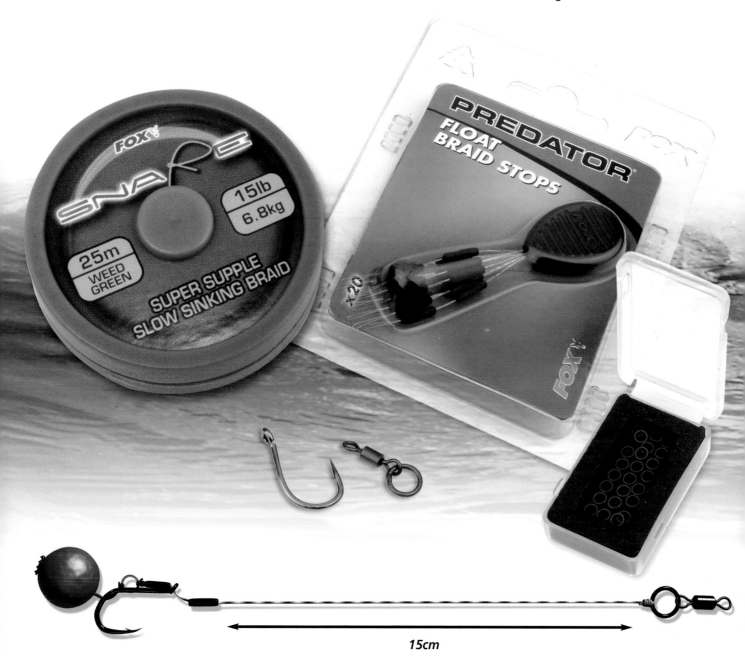

15cm

1. First pass the hooklink twice through the rig ring and attach it to the 25lb Snare using a 3-turn Grinner Knot.

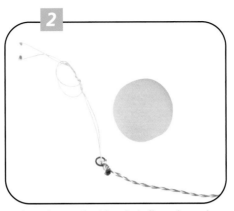

2. Thread some braid or bait floss through the rig ring and form a loop roughly the same diameter as the hookbait you will be using.

3. Now thread one of the Float Braid Stops onto the Snare and position it next to the rig ring.

4. Pass the end of the Snare down through the eye of the hook and thread it down so the rubber stop is next to the eye of the hook.

5. Now thread the second rubber Float Braid Stop onto the hooklink and slide it down to near the hook.

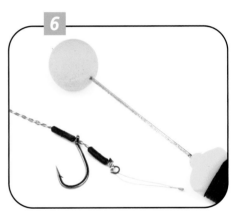

6. Pierce your hookbait with a lip-close baiting needle.

7. Mount the bait on the braid or floss and add a boilie prop.

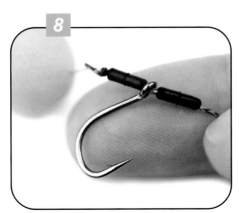

8. Adjust the two float stops so that they sit a few millimetres apart yet allow the hook to rotate freely around the hooklink.

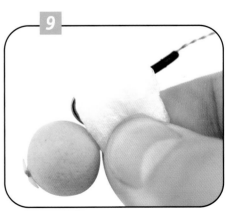

9. Prior to casting out, secure the 'hair' to the shank of the hook with a piece of High Riser Foam. This is important as it minimises the chance of tangles on the cast.

On many of the hard fished waters and day ticket lakes, carp have become adept at picking up the hookbait, testing for movement and feeling for the weight of the lead. You can help overcome this caution in four ways:

1. By using a longer hair…
2. A smaller hook…
3. A long braided hooklink…
4. And a running lead.

This next rig is well worth a go on waters where you think the fish may be picking up your hookbait and testing it against the free offerings.
They may also be feeling for the lead. In circumstances like these you may not get even the slightest indication at your end of the line that a fish is showing an interest. Similarly, if you are witnessing a lot of action over your hookbaits but not getting runs, it could be that the fish are wary of your rig or that your End Zone is not sufficiently disguised.

To tie this very simple rig, which we have christened the Ultra Confidence Rig, you will need the following items: 25lb Snare hooklink material from the Linx range, a size 8 Fox Arma Point LSC hook, a small buoyancy aid such as foam or artificial pop-up maize, a Flexi Ring Swivel and some Hi-SG Tungsten Putty.

1. First tie a loop in one end of the Snare to hold the hookbait.

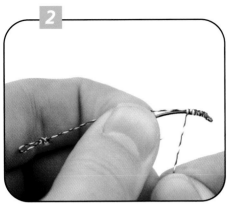

2. Thread the other end of the Snare down through the eye of the hook and, leaving a long hair section of about 5-6cm, form the knotless knot using eight turns around the hook shank.

3. Attach the size 7 Flexi ring Swivel to the other end of the hooklink. The overall length of the hooklink from swivel to eye of the hook should be between 30-35cm.

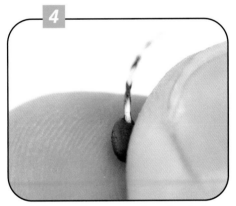

4. Add four or five 'mouse droppings' of High-SG Putty at evenly spaced intervals along the hooklink. This will keep it pinned down to the lakebed.

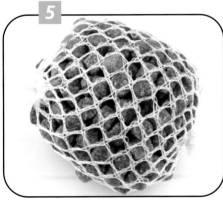

5. Make up a small PVA mesh parcel of pellets, boilie crumb and small boilie chops using the narrow Network Micromesh PVA or the Micro Stick PVA (see Chapter 8).

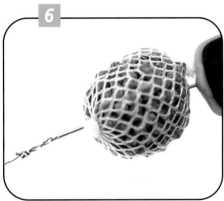

6. Gently ease a lip close baiting needle through the middle of the PVA parcel.

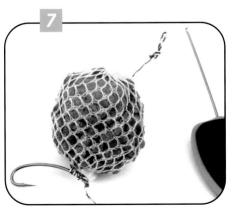

7. Catch the boilie loop at the end of the hair. Pull the loop through the PVA mesh and contents.

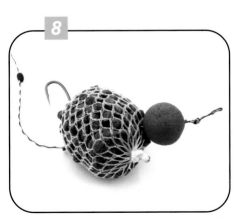

8. Add a small hookbait such as a couple of mini boilies, or a pellet hookbait.

9. Now add the buoyant item such as a piece of rig foam.

For the Ultra Confidence rig to work properly it must be fished with the right set-up; in particular a running lead. As the fish you are targeting are wary, it is important to ensure as much of the end zone is pinned to the lake bed as possible, so we incorporate some leadcore into the rig.

Here's the running lead set-up we would use with the ultra-confidence rig. You will need the following items: 45lb Leadcore, a Splicing Needle, Knot Protector bead, Camo Flexi bead and a swivel lead of you choice (here we have used a Tri-Bomb).

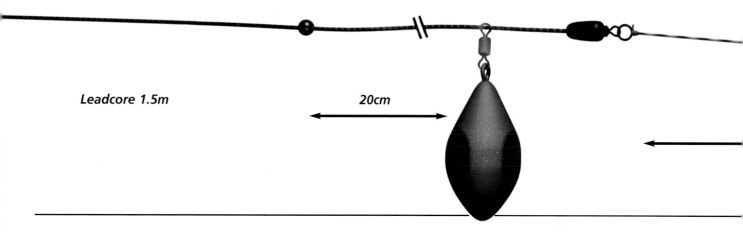

Leadcore 1.5m          20cm

!. Take a 1.5m length of leadcore and strip out a few cm of the lead.

2. Tie the Flexi Ring Swivel to the leadcore using a three turn blood knot.

3. At the other end of the leadcore splice in a loop.

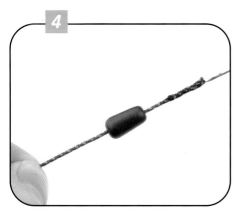

4. Using a lip-close baiting needle, thread a Knot Protector Bead onto the leadcore and bring it down so that it protects the knot where the leadcore joins the swivel.

5. Add the swivel lead that best suits the conditions, range and underwater profile of the lake you are fishing.

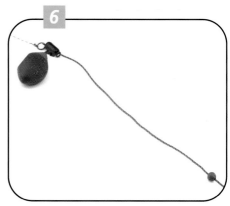

6. Next add a Rubber Flexi Bead to the leadcore and slide it down until it is positioned some 20cm behind the lead. Finally attach your main line to the loop in the end of the leadcore using a Loop-to-Loop Knot.

In practice the rig promotes confident feeding because the carp should be totally unaware of the dangers posed by the hookbait.

Once the rig enters the water the PVA mesh contents will spread slightly as the PVA melts covering the hook and the hair with just the hookbait being visible, sitting on top of a little pile of pellets, crumb and chops. Secondly the long hair allows greater degree of flexibility and movement on the part of the hair

and the hook itself and is therefore less likely to arouse the suspicions of a feeding carp once it actually takes the hookbait into its mouth. The extra long hooklink also helps in this regard.

Finally, should the fish pick up the hookbait and then back off slowly, feeling for the lead, the running lead should present far less resistance than other lead set ups, thus encouraging the fish to move off confidently.

As it does so the lead comes up against the Flexi Bead causing a momentary increase in resistance and this is all that is required to achieve the initial pricking that will in turn generate the run. Please note that the Flexi Bead will run easily along the leadcore so you can rest assured that the set-up is perfectly safe.

30-35cm

PVA mesh parcel. (Thread on with baiting needle and then add hookbaits)

Before we move on can we just show you a couple of neat ideas with the knotless knot? We have used the standard knotless knot throughout the book and the knot is probably used in 90% of modern carp rigs. However, there are one or two little tweaks you can experiment with if you find that takes are drying up on your water. They don't take a lot of explaining but they could make a big difference! Both are simple variations on the basic knotless knot that bring the hair section of the knot away from the hook shank in different ways.

The first variation we are going to look at is the stand off hair. The idea is when you attach the hookbait to the hook it tends to get pushed away slightly. This leads to more effective pricking as the hook is more likely to exit the mouth point downwards taking up a light hold in the bottom lip.

Here's how you tie it:

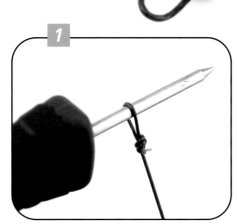

*1.First tie your boilie loop as usual.*

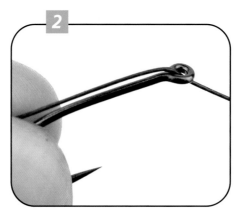

*2. Start to form the standard knot by threading the other end of the hooklink down through the eye of the hook.*

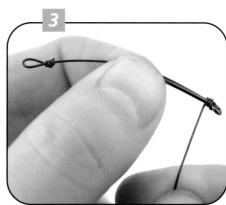

*3. Begin whipping the turns along the shank of the hook.*

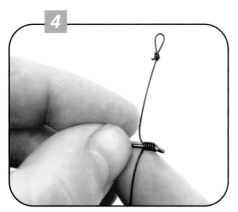

*4. After five turns fold the hair so that it sits at a right angle to the shank.*

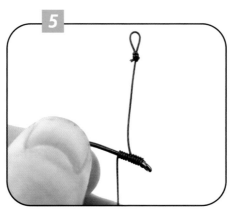

*5. Continue whipping another five turns on the other side of the hair. You will note that when you tighten up the hair stands off the hook at quite a sharp angle.*

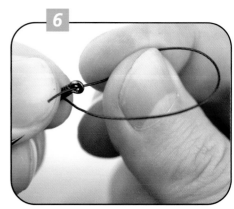

*6. Finish the knot by taking the tag end back down through the eye of the hook.*

FOX

As the name suggests, the Reverse Hair reverses the position of the bait compared to the conventional knotless knot presentation. Tying the Reverse Hair kicks the bait out from the hook creating a more aggressive angle. Again this works well simply because it can be harder for the fish to eject as the hook exits the mouth eye first and point down.

The Reverse Hair works equally well with bottom baits and pop-ups, however, if using with a pop-up it is best used over clean lake beds and not silt, weed or chod as the hook point can get covered with debris. Here's how you tie it:

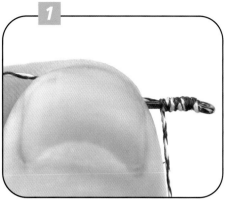

*1. Tie a small loop in the end of the braid then whip it to the shank of the hook (whipping away from the eye of the hook) .*

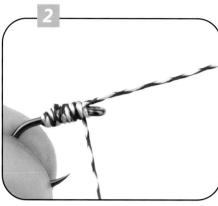

*2. Then fold the hair back along the shank so that it points away from the bend of the hook then whip five more turns over it .*

*3. Take the end of the braid back down through the eye to complete the knot.*

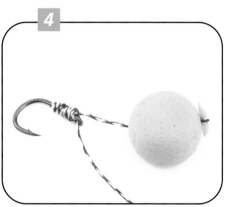

*4. Place the hookbait on the hair with a lip close baiting needle and secure with a boilie prop*

*5. Prior to casting secure the hair to the hooklink using some PVA Tape or string to prevent tangles.*

The word 'reverse' has cropped up once or twice already in this chapter and it's about to do so again. You see, many anglers seem to think that rigs have gone as far as they can go - you won't be surprised to hear that we don't subscribe to that view - and so they find themselves up against the wall of a dead end street, unable to move forward and at a loss what to do next. However, a few of the UK's best rig specialists starting looking at rigs from a different perspective, turning certain rig ideas on their heads, with the result that several very innovative rigs have been developed. We've already looked at the reverse Snowman and the Reverse Hair. Well, to close this chapter here's the Reverse Combi Rig.

In effect this is nothing more than an ordinary short stiff rig with an extra long hinge. In the Reverse Combi the hinge is created using soft, supple braid, whereas with the standard stiff rig the hinge is formed by the loop at the swivel. We all know how effective the original stiff rig can be but this rig simply takes it on another step in terms of suppleness. As with all stiff nylon presentations, the whole idea is that the stiffness makes the rig very difficult for the carp to eject. The braided section of the rig does not reduce this quality in any way, if anything it increases it! Because the whole rig is more supple, the carp are confronted with a whole new different ball game compared to the standard stiff rig.

This is what you'll need: A section of 25lb Rigidity Stiff Rig Material a size 4 Fox Arma Point SSBP hook, a piece of shrink tube, a length of 25lb Snare and a size 7 Flexi Ring Swivel.

20cm

1. First tie a loop in the end of the Rigidity and form the knotless knot. Keep the length of the hair fairly short so that the hookbait will sit quite tight to the hook.

2. Place the shrink tube on the Rigidity and position it over the knot before shrinking it into place over the steam from a boiling kettle.*

3. Using the knot shown right, attach the Rigidity hooklink to a 20cm length of the Snare.

4. To secure the knot dab a spot of Knotlok rig glue.

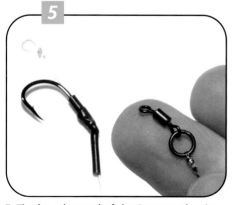

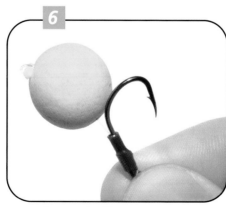

5. Tie the other end of the Snare to the ring in the Flexi Swivel.

6. Attach a standard bottom bait to the hair.

## Albright Knot

The following knot is ideal for joining two different types of material such as mainline to shock leader or stiff nylon and braid as shown below. The finished knot is extremely strong but is neat, compact and very unobtrusive.

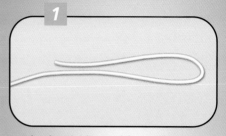

1. Take the Rigidity and form a loop.

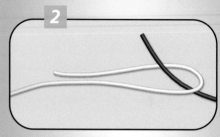

2. Thread the braid through the loop.

3. Working away from the loop, whip the braid around the Rigidity 10 times.

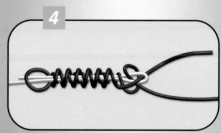

4. Whip six more turns working back towards the loop, then pass the tag end back down through the loop.

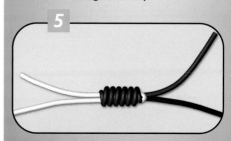

5. Pull the knot tight moistening prior to and during the process. The knot will have two tag ends. A dab of glue can be added for extra security.

* This operation should not be attempted by children under the age of 16 unless supervised by an adult.

# CHAPTER 8

*Chilly's Thoughts On Bait*

I don't know about you lot but talk of splitting enzymes, amino acids and other pearls of the bait making science normally puts me to sleep! For sure there are some baits that are better than others for one reason or another. The bottom line for me these days is that what I am using is (a) good for the fish and (b) they like to eat it. It is no secret that I use Mainline baits for nearly all my carp fishing these days. I have to deal with Kevin Knight on a fairly regular basis and it was obvious from the beginning some 15 years ago that my thoughts on bait were similar to his. Not being blinded by science I could concentrate on using that bait to best effect, and what I learnt was a real eye opener, I can tell you.

I have many thoughts on bait floating around in my head, but every time I really examine what I want to use bait for and what I want to achieve, I come back to the same conclusion. I want a bait that the carp will keep on eating because they enjoy it and it is doing them good. The up side of using a bait like this is that they will continue to lower their natural defences and in doing so become infinitely more catchable. To achieve this level of preoccupation, however, requires a lot of hard work and this is a phrase that some anglers shy away from. Not to put too fine a point on it, if you are not prepared to apply a bait properly, then no matter how good it is you will struggle to get the best from it. And therein lies the first hurdle.

You have to weigh up the kind of fishing you will be doing. How much time have you got at your disposal? How much can you afford to use? How much pressure are the carp under that you want to fish for, and how many are there? What bait(s) have been successful in the past? How much bait are the carp seeing? Plus a whole host of other things to consider. Once you have established the parameters under which you will be fishing you will be able to make a more informed choice.

Boillies are my preferred choice of carp bait. I back these up with other known carp catchers from time to time, but for now I want to look at the good old boillie. Shelf life boillies really have no place in my carp fishing.

Now that is a bit of a statement, and one that I suspect many will disagree with. For years I have been applying boillies to waters, and I can tell you that the higher the food quality of the bait the longer will be its life span in terms of catching carp. Ready mades are designed in the main to get the attention of the carp, and by having high levels of attraction elicit a feeding response. The trouble is, in my experience, it does not take long for the carp to suss out that they lack the quality to maintain a healthy life style. For 'shelf lifes' I read 'attractor baits' and I am sure that it is this high level of attraction that makes it so easy for the carp to recognise the dangers. In saying that, they do have a place. For the angler who is working on a very limited time budget they can prove invaluable. All you are looking for here is a bite in a short space of time. You need to get their attention quickly and ready mades do that very nicely.

Carp eat food! Of that there is little doubt. The better quality that food is, the more good it will do the fish and the more likely he is to eat it.
The longer stay angler or one that can visit his venue on a regular basis needs to take this into account. I think it only fair to say that I have much more time than most and I am looking to apply a bait for the long term. I am not fazed if it takes some time for the fish to respond, the bait I use is good and I know that they will eventually switch on to it.

More often than not though, I don't have to wait too long. I have been using Mainline baits for 15 years now and they seem to have the ability to produce baits that have instant appeal but also ones that last as long as I want them to. From the Grange to the new Fusion, I have always found that the carp love it and will get caught time and time again on it because they know it is good for them. You will have to find a bait that you are confident in and one that the fish want to eat, and then set about making it available to them as often as possible. Remember, the more they see of it without getting caught on it, the more confident they will be. The more confident they are the more likely you are to catch them.

## CHAPTER 8. CHILLY'S THOUGHTS ON BAIT

Some of you will no doubt have read about the amount of bait that I use from time to time. And, no doubt, some of you will be saying, "well its alright for him, he gets it for free". I'll not dispute that, but the reason I test baits for Mainline is to find out how effective their baits are and what we can and can't get away with. Carp eat food and lots of it! I think it would surprise a great many anglers just how much a carp can eat in a single sitting. Many of you will just have to take my word for that. By knowing that fact you can adjust your own fishing accordingly. I often use this analogy to put my point across. Formula one racing drivers roar around racetracks in the latest high tech cars. Something the average driver will never do. Much of the reason the car companies plough so much money into this sport, is that they can transfer much of the data and technology into the cars that we drive on the roads. It doesn't mean that you can drive around at 200mph; it just means that you are driving something reliable that won't let you down.

Whilst I would never consider myself as the Michael Schumacher of carp fishing, by writing about my findings it will hopefully give anglers a better understanding of the carp they are trying to catch. And the more you understand, the more likely you are to catch them. Knowledge is power!!

What a wonderful sales pitch it would be if I was to say that all you have to do is buy a ton of quality bait and throw it in the pond, sit back and start to reel them in.

Large quantities of bait work, but by far the most important aspect of bait application is the regularity with which you put it in and where you put it. All you have to do now is select the water you want to fish and the bait that you want to use. If the venue has a closed season then so much the better, because you will be applying bait with no angling pressure, their confidence will build up so much quicker. If the water remains open all year round, then you will be establishing it whilst you are fishing. I try and get bait into as many of the productive spots that I can. By doing this I am not too bothered if one of the spots is being fished, because hopefully one of the others will not. Even if you have to fish an area that you have not baited, hopefully by then they will recognise your bait wherever you put it. I am constantly amazed that anglers who for instance, can only fish weekends say they cannot compete with others who have more time. You can, but it takes a little sacrifice. If you can only fish say a Friday and Saturday night, there is a way of increasing your session. Instead of a visit to the pub on a Wednesday night why not go to the lake and put some bait in? Not lots, say fifty or sixty baits on your chosen spots. That bait is then working for you until you arrive. The session is now four days long. If you can do it every other day then you will have bait in the water all week long. There is no doubt in my mind that others will catch fish because of your hard work, but if you stick to it you will invariably get the lions share. It all depends on how much you want it.

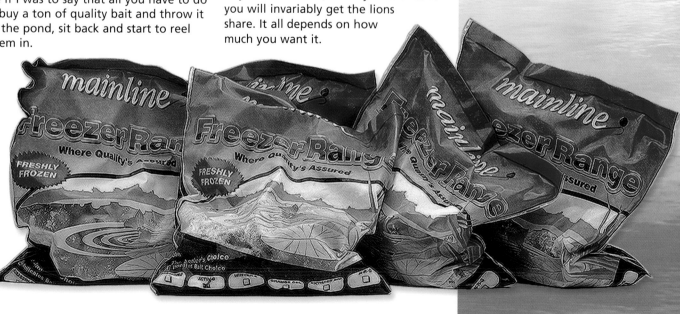

## CHAPTER 8. CHILLY'S THOUGHTS ON BAIT

I have been discussing boillies so far, because that is what I use the most. But I think it's worth considering what else is available. Lets start with pellets. You would have to have been living on another planet not to have noticed the impact they have had (and will continue to have) on carp fishing. In a word, carp love 'em! Much the same as the boillie, they simply need to be introduced to spots on a regular basis. They are quite inexpensive and sometimes this can mean that everyone is using them. Carp will continue to be caught by their use, but sometimes we need to give them a little bit of a helping hand. Once again Mainline have come to my aid. They provide Response Pellets that carry the flavour or more precisely the food signal of the boillies I am using. These have proved a massive edge for me and have given my baiting a new dimension.

If you are using someone else's pellet then I would suggest you get hold of some low fat trout pellet (they seem to absorb more liquids) and coat them in the flavours/attractors you are using. Leave them for a day or two to fully take on the liquids, and hey presto you have a pellet carrying the same signal as your bait. For those on a low budget, it's an ideal and cheap way of baiting up.

Particle baits again need little in the way of introduction. Probably the most popular is hemp. I will use this as the main example, but it's best not to forget other seeds. Most notable amongst those for me would be Hinder's Parti-Blend. I also include maggots and casters in this list, but if you are on a budget then their long-term use may be a burden on your pocket. First and foremost as with any nut or seed, they need to be prepared properly. In general most seeds will need soaking for at least 24 hrs and boiled for between 20 and 30 minutes. This ensures that they are not harmful to the carp, and secondly they are infinitely more attractive and edible once they have been soaked and boiled. The process releases their natural oils, sugars and flavours. Hemp is one of the most awesome carp attractors of all time. Its use often results in the carp becoming totally pre-occupied on it, which in many respects is what we are trying to achieve. The down side of this can be that it's difficult to get a bite when using other baits over the top of it. One thing is for sure though, if you want to get carp in your swim and keep them there then hemp will do just that. Cheap and easy to prepare. I find it best when used in conjunction with other baits. My favourites being boillies and pellet. Hemp is very instantaneous and needs little in the way of pre-baiting, but it is still a good idea to introduce some onto

your spots as often as you can. Make sure that you introduce some larger food items at the same time just to get them used to seeing and eating it.

I have always viewed nuts with a certain amount of suspicion. There is no doubt that carp absolutely love them. Used in moderation there is little that can go wrong but because they are classed as a particle bait, they tend to be applied at needless levels. In extreme cases their excessive use on some waters has lead to fish loosing weight and becoming out of condition, so please be careful when using them. Nuts I usually soak for 48 hours before boiling for a minimum of 30 minutes. Over the years I have used several different nuts but the main two that stick out above the rest are tiger nuts and peanuts. As my paranoia about nuts continued, I dropped my use of peanuts. I have seen no evidence that they do any harm, but I don't think they do the fish much good either. Tigers really are a bit of a conundrum in that if they do not do the carp much good then why do they keep on eating them? I have no definitive answer but I suspect it's a little like kids with sweets. They simply like the taste and texture. One of the main drawbacks is that they can sometimes become a never-ending baiting cycle. The carp wolf them down, barely pausing to chew them.

They then go somewhere else in the lake and excrete whole and partially chewed tigers. Along comes another group of carp and the whole cycle is repeated. They feel as if they have eaten a meal but have got very little out of it. Consequently the fish loose condition and very rarely put on any weight. By way of an example look at what has happened at CEMEX Anglings Horton Church Lake. The use of any nuts has been banned, and for the last two years the carp have once again been piling on the weight. So for me the only nut I now use is a tiger if I think I need to, and that situation rarely happens these days. If you are going to use and pre-bait with them then please use as little as possible.

Well there you have it. My thoughts on bait. There are obviously some omissions here but I can only talk about the baits that I have used. To do otherwise would be pure speculation on my part. As I said at the beginning, boillies and pellet are my preferred choice but they are by no means the only option. I have given some cheaper options and I hope that they have helped. Bait is just one part of the carp fishing jigsaw puzzle. A good bait helps but it still needs to be applied correctly in the right areas. One thing I have found for sure is that there is nothing to beat quality and carp know a quality bait when they see one.

## ***CHAPTER 9***

*PVA And High Riser Tricks*

One of the most significant advances in carp fishing in the last few years has been the development of more specialised varieties of dissolving material such as PVA and High Riser Soluble Foam. There's so many different kinds around these days it's difficult to know where to start! What with PVA string, tape, bags, mesh and micromesh, it's small wonder we get confused at times. In addition the varied tactics that can be employed when using these products have multiplied tenfold and to be honest there is enough material at hand to fill a book simply on PVA alone!

However, we don't have enough space here to write such a book so we will have to be satisfied with a brief yet detailed look at several presentations that involve the use of PVA string, tape, mesh (including micromesh) and bags.

## "there is enough material at hand to fill a book simply on PVA alone!"

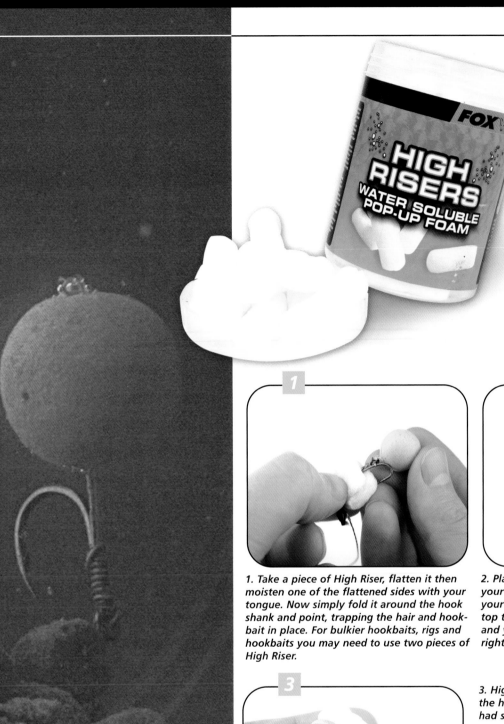

We'll kick off with a few little tricks you can use with our High Riser dissolving foam. Tangles can be a pain in the backside and we have all been plagued by them at one time or another, especially if we are using braided hooklinks, which are much more likely to tangle on the cast than nylon hooklinks or stiff rigs.
One of the many uses that soluble foam can be put to is preventing tangles and here are a few suggestions for you:

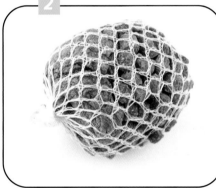

1. Take a piece of High Riser, flatten it then moisten one of the flattened sides with your tongue. Now simply fold it around the hook shank and point, trapping the hair and hookbait in place. For bulkier hookbaits, rigs and hookbaits you may need to use two pieces of High Riser.

2. Place one or two pieces of loose foam into your PVA bags or mesh parcels along with your pellets etc. When the foam floats to the top that will tell you that the bag has melted and you can check that it is lying in the right place.

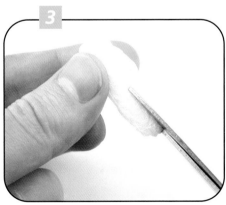

3. High Riser was originally intended to keep the hookbait off the bottom until the lead had settled. This is particularly useful fishing over weed or soft silt. Take several pieces of foam and cut them half way through along their length using scissors. Dampen the cut with saliva before placing four or five pieces of foam along the hooklink. This makes the rig virtually 100% tangle proof. In addition the foam makes the perfect target for free offerings or spods when it floats to the surface. The foam tends to come up a piece at a time so you can keep hitting the right spot until all the foam has surfaced.

The first type of bait presentation that utilised PVA was the Stringer. The method was developed in the early eighties by carp fishing pioneers such as Rod Hutchinson. Although twenty years old, the Stringer is still one of the most effective ways of presenting a number of baits close to the hook. In addition, the use of a stringer virtually eliminates tangles on the cast.

All that is needed to make a stringer is a long needle and 10mm Fox PVA Tape. This tape has a multitude of carp fishing uses but the 10mm width makes it ideal for creating stringers: the profile of the tape keeps the baits separated and no knots are needed to secure the baits in place. This optimum performance is largely due to the embossed, textured surface which is also used on our Fade Away PVA bags.

*Now for some ideas for stringers using PVA tape and string:*

*1. To make a standard stringer thread four or five baits onto a stringer needle.*

*2. Place the tape in the crook of the stringer needle and thread the baits on to the tape*

*3. Leave a space between each of the baits to ensure the PVA breaks down.*

*4. Slide the point of the hook through the tape*

*5. The finished stringer looks like this, and ensures a series of free offerings are close to the hookbait.*

Although the basic Stringer is highly effective there are countless tips, tricks and variations which can give a slight edge on hard fished waters. In fact, the only limit to these variations is your imagination.

Remember, carp are creatures of habit and once they start getting caught on a certain presentation they will soon come to associate it with danger. Experimentation is the name of the game and the list of possibilities is endless. Firstly, when casting into weedy swims some of the tape can be wrapped around the hook point to mask and protect it on descent.

## Here are a few more suggestions for you to try:

*A very handy trick is to cut each bait in half after they have been threaded onto the tape. When the tape melts a string of half baits will be left close to the hookbait. This also allows a quicker release of flavour and attraction from the heart of each cut boilie.*

*Stringers are invariably attached in such a way that they present a line of baits close to the hookbait. An effective alternative is to attach the end of the stringer to the hook point creating a neat pile of freebies that looks quite different to the norm.*

*Using double hookbaits? Then why not make up a batch of double freebies? Tie them in pairs like this using PVA tape and introduce them with a catapult. The tape on the outside will melt quickly but the PVA in the middle of the baits will not melt and the free offerings will be presented on the lakebed as individual pairs, just like your hookbait. The carp will soon get used to finding double freebies and this will reduce suspicion.*

*Why stop at a single stringer? You can tie two or even three separate stringers to the hook if you like. Tie the last bait to the stringer with a couple of overhand knots.*

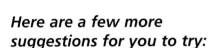

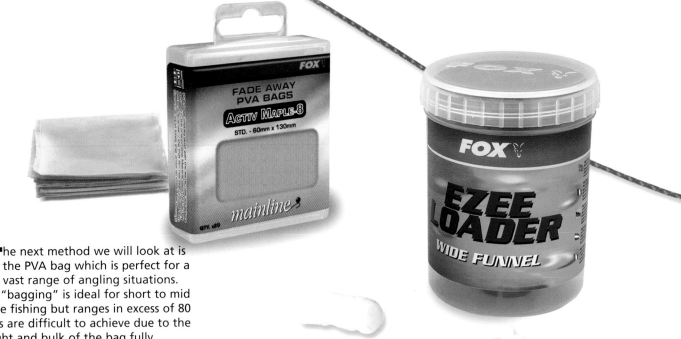

The next method we will look at is the PVA bag which is perfect for a vast range of angling situations. PVA "bagging" is ideal for short to mid range fishing but ranges in excess of 80 yards are difficult to achieve due to the weight and bulk of the bag fully loaded. To use PVA at longer range there are other techniques which we will look at later in the chapter.

Fox Fade Away PVA is a solid, non-porous film which, unlike mesh, allows the addition of oil based liquid attractors.

Fox Fade Away PVA bags are available in two differing thicknesses to suit conditions. The 38 micron bags are ideal for all round use and winter; the thinner film helping the bag to disperse quickly in the coldest of water temperatures. The heavier gauge 50 micron bags provide a slower melt rate and are designed for deeper water in summer water temperatures. This heavier film ensures that the bag reaches the bottom intact without melting on descent – a common problem with thinner, lighter bags that can result in a wide spread of bait. As a guide use the 38 micron bags for winter fishing and for summer work in depths no greater than 3 metres, and the 50 micron bags for summer use in water depths exceeding 3 metres and for distance casting where extra bag strength is required.

In addition to different thicknesses, Fade Away bags come in two widths, 60mm and 70mm. Obviously the larger bags can hold more bait but can't be cast quite as far as the narrower model.

To start off with we will look at the basic method of creating a PVA bag. It employs our Ezee Loader to great effect!

1. First insert the funnel provided into the bag

2. Place the lead weight in the little cup at the mouth of the funnel.

3. Now locate the baited hair and hooklink in the bag so that it sits at the bottom. The hooklink should run through the slot.

4. Next top up the bag with the bait you wish to use. It could be a bag mix, boilie chops, groundbait, crumb or pellets. Fill the bag until it is 3/4 full.

5. Now add a piece of PVA foam. This isn't essential but provides a useful reference to show when the bag has dissolved.

6. Drop the lead down the funnel so that it rests on top of the contents.

7. Carefully remove the filled PVA bag and ease the main line out through the slot in the side of the Ezee Loader.

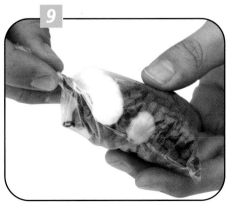

8. Using a cotton bud dampen the insides of the bag.

9. Twist the top of the bag around your tubing or leadcore. (Note: If you are using stiff tubing you can suck any excess air out of the bag to create a more solid, streamlined bag.)

10. For added security tie off the neck of the bag to the tubing using our PVA Tape.

Standard PVA bags are fine for fishing at distances up to 80 yards but for longer distances you need to use smaller more streamlined bags, such as the Fox Bullet bags. To achieve maximum distances the finished bags need to be as compact as possible and the lead needs to be positioned at the bottom of the bag, not at the top.

If you intend to fish PVA bags at range you also need to use the right rigs. Helicopter rigs are ideal for bag fishing and it is a good idea to keep your hook link as short as you can. You may think that 10cm sounds too short but when you think about it, the hook bait will fit neatly in the PVA bag and once the PVA has melted, the hook bait will be surrounded by a tight group of free offerings. A feeding carp will not move off at all when eating the contents of the bag and the short hook link provides maximum shock effect, ensuring a positive indication and run.

For a Helicopter set-up here's how to create the ideal PVA bag:

## *"for longer distances you need to use smaller more stream-lined bags"*

1. Add a piece of High Riser foam to the point of the hook.

2. First place the lead in the tapered end of the bag, (Ensuring the hook length and bait are kept outside the bag).

3. Three quarter fill the bag with your favourite bait. You can use an Ezee Loader for this.

4. The hooklink should lie along the bag with the hookbait at the top of the bag.

5. Squeeze the bag to remove as much air as possible, at the same time twisting the bag around the lead.

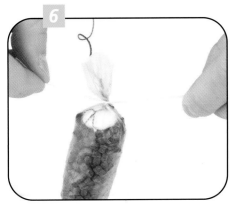

6. Secure with a knot of PVA Tape.

7. Fold the corners of the bag back upon themselves and dampen them slightly.

8. Stick the corners to the side of the bag. Take care not to put too much moisture onto the corners or they will melt the bag. You should aim to make the bag as tight and compact as possible so as to increase casting distance.

The PVA stick has become one of the most popular PVA techniques since it rose to prominence a few years ago. Like all PVA methods, the stick can prove deadly as it delivers a packet of loose feed on or around the hook bait. Between them, the Fox consultants get through miles of PVA tubing; such is the effectiveness of the method.

The whole method revolves around a simple "Funnel and Plunger" system which creates a tube of compacted bait. In the Fox range, there are two sizes of plunger available, narrow and wide which measure 25mm and 40mm in diameter respectively. The larger size is ideal for introducing bigger quantities of bait when targeting numbers of fish and aiming for multiple catches. Repeated regular casting to the same area can be a very effective tactic on busy venues, especially when combined with light and accurate spodding. In addition to the two diameters there are two varieties of PVA: Fine and Heavy. The Fine mesh has a fast dissolve time, even in the coldest of lakes. It's tight weave makes it perfect for use with small items such as micro pellet and maggot.

The Heavy mesh has a slower dissolve time and is therefore more suited to use during the warmer months. It is also more suited to use with larger items such as boilies and big pellets.

Although the method we look at here relies on mounting the finished stick on the rig or hook, there are countless other uses for the mesh. The shape and weight of the finished stick means they can be fired greater distances with a catapult than could ever be achieved with loose feed alone. Introducing a number of loose sticks can prove to be highly effective as the fish get used to finding piles of bait and are less likely to be suspicious of the one containing the hook bait.

The Funnel and Plunger is also ideal for creating small parcels of chum mixers when floater fishing. To create some additional weight for catapulting, it is a good idea to add a few small stones to the bottom of the bag.

*Fine PVA Funnel Mesh*

*Heavy PVA Funnel Mesh*

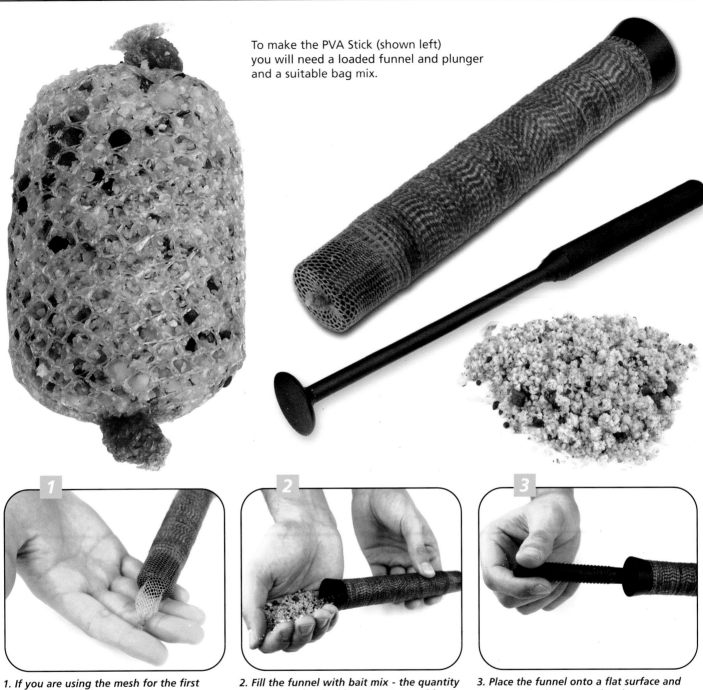

To make the PVA Stick (shown left) you will need a loaded funnel and plunger and a suitable bag mix.

1. If you are using the mesh for the first time tie a knot in the end of the mesh.

2. Fill the funnel with bait mix - the quantity dictates the finished bag size. As a guide, the greater the casting distance the smaller the bag should be.

3. Place the funnel onto a flat surface and compress the bait using the plunger.

4. This process creates a compact package that casts well, sinks quickly and breaks apart effectively on the lakebed.

5. Grasp the mesh immediately above the contents and twist, trapping the contents as tightly as possible within the mesh.

6. Cut the bag away and tie a second overhand knot in the end of the PVA - this becomes the base of the next bag you produce.

One of the big advantages of using mesh and PVA bags is that you can make loads of individual parcels of bait up in advance of your session. The simplest method of attaching a stick or PVA bag is to simply hook it to the rig to release a concentrated cluster of attractors immediately around the hook bait.

For long range casting and deep or weedy venues, a good method is to thread the stick onto the rig. There are very few limitations to the rig you use but it is a good idea to try and incorporate a Kwik Change Swivel and Sleeve which have been designed to allow parcels and PVA bags to be loaded straight onto hook links. The Kwik Change swivel features a uniquely designed eye shape which is partially open with a small lead in. Attaching the hook length is simple: tie a small loop in the end of the hook link; placing it over the "V" before securing it in place with the purpose made tapered sleeve.

The rig we use in the example below is the 360 rig described in Chapter 2. We have used an in-line lead and a leadcore leader but with a size 7 Kwik Change Swivel spliced to one end.

Here's how you attach the stick:

*Always use a a Kwik Change Swivel when using PVA sticks, particularly on prolific venues.*

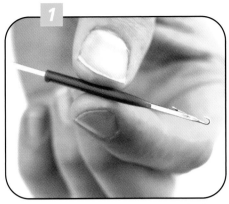

1. Thread the anti-tangle sleeve supplied with the Kwik Change Swivel onto a Lip Close needle.

2. Thread the needle through the edge of the stick. Do not try and go through the full length of the stick.

3. Place the loop in the hook length over the crook in the needle before pulling it back through the stick.

4. Secure the hook in the end of the stick. To prevent the hook point being masked it is a good idea to add very fine groundbait to the first 10mm of the bag before filling with larger coarser bait.

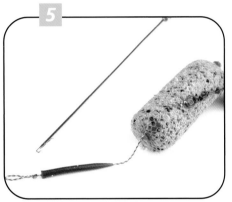

5. Thread the sleeve off the needle and on to the hook length.

6. Simply hook the loop on to the Kwik Change swivel then slide the sleeve over the loop to secure it in place.

One of the main advantages of this method is that it allows bags or mesh sticks to be made up in advance and for hooklinks to be pre-tied for the ultimate in convenience. This proves invaluable on venues where lots of action is encountered; simply unclip the rig, thread it up inside another stick, clip it back on and cast out!

Multiple spare sticks or bags with the hooklink already threaded and hookbait attached can even be made up in advance and stored in a bucket. Each time a fish is caught or a cast is made, simply clip a new one on and you are ready to go.

Over the past five years PVA techniques have come on in leaps and bounds and are continuing to evolve. There are certain anglers out there, including some of the Fox consultants, who have taken PVA fishing to the next level and developed it in to something of an art form. Here we will look at what we believe is one of the ultimate bag rigs.

For the rig to work properly it must be used in conjunction with an in-line lead, and the flat sides of the In-line Flat Pear and Kling-On are particularly effective. While we are on the subject of leads it is worth thinking about the size of lead used with PVA bags. A 2.25oz lead may seem light but it is always worth considering what the overall weight of the packed PVA bag will be when finished. Obviously the weight of the bag doesn't just depend on the weight of the lead but also on the type of bait, the size of the bag and how full it is. As an example: the bullet bag we are about to create with a 2.25oz lead and pellet weighs exactly four ounces. Always think about what test curve your rods can cast and take this into consideration when choosing a lead and filling a PVA bag.

1. Place the lead in the base of the PVA Bag keeping the hook on the outside.

2. Fill the bag keeping the hook and bait outside the bag.

3. When the bag is full, place the hook bait on top.

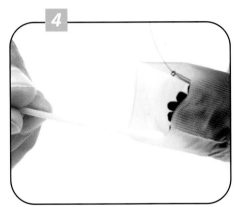

4. Using a cotton bud moisten the inside of the bag.

5. Twist the PVA around the tubing taking care to remove as much air as possible.

6. Once the bag is completed suck as much air as you can from inside the bag using the rigid tubing.

The finished bag is small and compact; sucking the air out of the bag creates a solid vacuum packed unit that is highly aerodynamic. Loading the lead at the front of the bag ensures it is nose heavy and the bag casts incredibly well.

In the example shown here we used a bullet bag, but the technique can be used with any Fade Away PVA bag. As we said at the start of the chapter, we could write a book on PVA alone. Hopefully what we have covered in the chapter has been food for thought and will give you a good basis of ideas that you can tailor to the waters you fish.

**M**ounting a stick on a hooklink is a fantastic way of eliminating tangles at all casting ranges. However, as with any rig, when fishing a stick at long-range it is always worth taking a few precautions to make sure when the end zone reaches the lake or river bed, the hook bait and rig are presented correctly. There is nothing more soul destroying than reeling in a rod that has been left out overnight to find the end zone in a tangle. PVA sticks keep the hooklink straight and under tension, making tangles completely impossible.

After lots of trial and error, the Fox consultants have found the following rig to be a most effective "Stick rig" for distance fishing. The rig is a helicopter style set-up which provides excellent anti-tangle properties. Such is the effectiveness of the rig, Fox consultant Andy Little uses it for barbel, bream and tench fishing as well as carp fishing. This 14lb 4oz barbel from the River Wey in Surrey fell to a Halibut Pellet fished over a stick of ground pellet. Here's how we make the rig:

*"This rig is equally effective for Tench, Barbel and Bream"*

*3. Finally, tie the rig to the swivel. Here we have used a simple knotless knot presentation tied to 150mm of Coretex coated hooklink material.*

*1. Take a 30cm length of Fox Lead Core and splice a size 7 swivel to one end and a loop in the other.*

*2. Mount an in-line lead of your choice onto the lead core then add a rubber Flexi bead, Flexi ring swivel (placing the ring of the swivel onto the leadcore) and another Flexi bead.*

1. Construct a 90mm PVA stick as you would normally but leave a length of PVA behind the knot.

2. Thread the loose PVA through the swivel in the nose of the lead.

3. Knot the stick to the rig using a simple overhand knot before trimming with a pair of braid blades.

4. The rig should now be looking like this. The length of the bag and the hook length is important as the hook should be level with the end of the bag, keeping the hooklink extended.

5. Place the hook in the end of the stick.

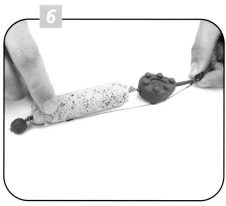

6. Slight adjustments can be made to how the rig sits by moving the bottom bead up the lead core slightly.

The finished rig hangs like this when ready to cast. Mounting the stick in the way we do means the whole rig is extremely well balanced and casts like a dream. In the right hands, with the right equipment it is possible to cast this rig well over 100 yards. One other advantage is prior to adding the hook length, pre-made sticks can be cast out into the area creating a bed of bait.